To Bill and Gale Roberson

Who, despite the disappointment of unanswered prayer, press on believing, trusting, and knowing that God works all things together for good.

Foreword by ANNE GRAHAM LOTZ

WHY DOESN'T GOD *ANSWER* MY PRAYERS?

A BIBLICAL GUIDE *TO* GOD'S HIDDEN PURPOSES

ERWIN W. LUTZER

WITH SCOTT MACDONALD

MOODY PUBLISHERS

CHICAGO

All emphasis in Scripture has been added.

Portions of this book have been adapted from Dr. Erwin Lutzer's sermons on unanswered prayer.

Names and details of some stories have been changed to protect the privacy of individuals.

Edited by Amanda Cleary Eastep
Interior design: Kaylee Lockenour Dunn
Cover design: Studio Gearbox

Library of Congress Cataloging-in-Publication Data

Names: Lutzer, Erwin W. author
Title: Why doesn't God answer my prayers? : a biblical guide to God's hidden purposes / Erwin Lutzer ; with Scott MacDonald.
Description: [Chicago, IL] : [Moody Publishers], [2026] | Includes bibliographical references. | Summary: "Dr. Lutzer helps us see God's love and guidance even when He seems silent. This biblical guide hits on our most perplexing questions, like: When the person you love isn't healed. When the worst happens. When evil feels like it's winning. When promises are unfulfilled . . . and more"-- Provided by publisher.
Identifiers: LCCN 2025043551 (print) | LCCN 2025043552 (ebook) | ISBN 9780802438997 paperback | ISBN 9780802467751 ebook
Subjects: LCSH: Prayer--Biblical teaching | Presence of God--Biblical teaching | Hidden God--Biblical teaching | Bible--Criticism, interpretation, etc. | BISAC: RELIGION / Christian Living / Spiritual Growth | RELIGION / Christian Living / General
Classification: LCC BS680.P64 L88 2026 (print) | LCC BS680.P64 (ebook)
LC record available at https://lccn.loc.gov/2025043551
LC ebook record available at https://lccn.loc.gov/2025043552

Originally delivered by fleets of horse-drawn wagons, the affordable paperbacks from D. L. Moody's publishing house resourced the church and served everyday people. Now, after more than 125 years of publishing and ministry, Moody Publishers' mission remains the same—even if our delivery systems have changed a bit. For more information on other books (and resources) created from a biblical perspective, go to www.moodypublishers.com or write to:

Moody Publishers
820 N. LaSalle Boulevard
Chicago, IL 60610

3 5 7 9 10 8 6 4 2

Printed in the United States of America

Contents

Foreword

Dr. Erwin Lutzer has a pastor's heart. He genuinely cares about people. This book, *Why Doesn't God Answer My Prayers?*, breathes his compassionate understanding on every page. With biblical examples and personal anecdotes, Dr. Lutzer answers deep personal questions you and I may have asked at one time or another about our unanswered prayers.

The first time I remember meeting Dr. Lutzer was at our *Just Give Me Jesus* Chicago Revival kickoff that was held in Moody Church. He was the pastor at the time and greeted me warmly in the green room. On the platform, he gave his full support to our revival. From that moment forward, I considered him a friend.

I have been with him from time to time since then, most notably when I spoke at Moody's Founder's Week in 2018. Following the message, I was privileged to have lunch with Dr. Lutzer and the interim president of Moody Bible Institute, Greg Thornton. He questioned me about some of the pushback I have received as a woman in ministry, then once again, gave me his full support and blessing.

Since that time, once a year, he and his wife, Rebecca, arrange to have dinner with me so that our friendship has deepened. It was after our dinner in the fall of 2025 that he asked if I would write the foreword to *Why Doesn't God Answer My Prayers?* I was humbled to be asked, while at the same time eager to read the book and gain his wisdom regarding prayer. It has not disappointed.

From the very first chapter, he had my attention, as well as later in the book when he described our Lord's prayer in the garden of Gethsemane the night He was betrayed as being unanswered. Jesus, as our High Priest who ever lives to make intercession for us, understands firsthand the struggle of unanswered prayer.

Thank you, Dr. Lutzer, for caring enough about God's people to encourage all of us to trust Him more as we seek to move heaven through our prayers.

Anne Graham Lotz
International Speaker
Bestselling Author of *The Daniel Prayer* and
The Light of His Presence

The Purpose of This Book

The purpose of this book is not to answer every question you might have regarding the mysteries of prayer but rather to give you hope when your prayers are not answered, or at least when they aren't answered the way you expected. We must humbly confess that God has hidden plans that we may never comphehend. Yet, from Genesis to Revelation, God invites us to connect with Him regarding our needs, our hopes, and, yes, even our wants. How He answers might mystify us, but fellowship and worship are always the larger goal. We come to Him occupied with our need and leave our prayer time occupied with our God. And we have the promise that He rewards those who seek Him out.

I have three simple goals in this book.

First, I want to explain why God might not answer our requests. Indeed, as we shall see, we might be asking Him for things He has not promised to give us. Or, He might have His own reasons for withholding an answer because of a larger purpose He has in store for us. In fact, if you're like me, often when looking back you end up thanking God for unanswered prayer. We can't see around corners, but God can. Unanswered prayer can turn out to be a blessing.

Second, I hope to show how we frequently hinder our own prayers when we ask with wrong motives and, in the process, miss the whole point of what prayer is about. Knowingly or unknowingly, we can be the very reason why heaven appears silent.

Third, prayer is communication with God; I think we all agree on that. Yet I want to expand that definition to include giving God praise and looking at all of life through the lens of gratefulness. No matter who you are, your background, or how many days or years you've been walking with God, there are some prayers that are always appropriate; prayers of adoration that will glorify His name. Unanswered prayer is one of the ways in which God grows our faith, and in our disappointment, He intends that we seek Him more earnestly for comfort and fellowship. In other words, *despite unanswered prayer, I want you to be motivated to pray more, not less*!

In summary: My prayer is that when you finish reading this book, you will take a fresh look at prayer, trusting God's purposes, not your own. Prayer is God's gift to us, and we must return it to Him and bring Him glory, not merely seeking to have our needs met. I hope these pages help you take inventory of your prayer life, and as necessary, make appropriate adjustments.

Years ago, I preached a sermon series, "The Triumph of Unanswered Prayer." Since then, more needs to be said. With this book, I have expanded this material under this new title, *Why Doesn't God Answer My Prayers?* And along the way, we will discover why we must keep pursuing our relationship with God even when our prayers are seemingly unanswered.

Also, I received help writing this book from Scott MacDonald, a seminary professor who has had experience in the mission field. He is now teaching at the Canadian Baptist Theological Seminary and College in Cochrane, Alberta. We agree theologically, and in addition to assisting with the book as a whole, he specifically crafted the prayers for you to pray as you read. I wish him a great writing career in the future.

So, we write this book for anyone who asked of God and did not receive and the person who longs for God, whether or not their requests are answered. It is for the person who is angry with God; it is for those who are filled with doubt and discouragement and those who don't pray because they believe prayer has "no cash value" (in other words, it does little, if any, good).

By the end of this book, our hope is that you will discover a new paradigm for how to pray. As the Lord leads us into His Word, you will find fulfillment in your own individual prayer life because it leads to blessed fellowship with God. Lord willing, you will embrace God's hidden purposes in prayer, seeing that His agenda transcends much of what we ask of Him from our limited and temporal perspective. Even as we wonder why He doesn't answer our prayers, let us take time to seek Him through prayer!

Claiming Promises God Did Not Make

You can name it, but you can't claim it!

God has forsaken me!" That is a direct quote from a woman I knew who claimed healing for her husband, but when God did not grant the healing, she felt abandoned by Him. She had been listening to a so-called faith healer who insisted that physical healing could be *demanded* from God based on His promises.

This dear woman eventually came to realize that she had been deceived by a TV preacher who lived in luxury even as he told his followers that if they only had faith, they too could be healthy and wealthy. Because physical suffering is so debilitating, such teaching is attractive and gains a wide audience.

I once received a letter from a man I shall call Ted, who was incarcerated. He was trying to draw closer to God and had been given resources by various clergy that helped him grow in his walk as a Christian. However, some of the material he read preached "health and wealth." He explained:

> *I received a letter . . . that said there was power in my confession, and if I were to take authority over my situation and shout, "I am rich," blessings would come to me. I did this for several months, but I have not received any extra money. In fact, now the money from my commissary account is not arriving on time. I began confessing that I walk in divine health like their ministry instructs me to do, but then I discovered that my liver enzymes were off and other lab results were not encouraging.*

Fortunately, this man saw through the ruse and had the spiritual insight to pray differently. He continued:

> *I have since changed my prayers, and I now confess that I am only healed if God wants me to be. I struggle with whether these other ministries are of God. Please give me your advice on this. I am afraid of making false accusations about ministries that talk about Jesus and say they are anointed of God. I just know that their teaching does not work for me.*

These prayers did not work for Ted, and they quite likely do not work for millions of others. God did not intend them to work. We dare not insist God give us what He did not promise. To put it differently, we cannot claim promises that are not ours. Too many teachers, including some with television and internet followings, propound false doctrine. Of course we can pray for healing; we can pray for a miracle. And sometimes God grants our request. But God has not promised that we can simply "name it and claim it," insisting that it is always His will.

Where shall we look to find similar ideas? This particular false teaching has been around for a long time. A man by the name of William Kenyon (1867–1948) drew ideas from the Christian Science religion.[1] Christian Science was originally started by Mary Baker Eddy in the 1800s.[2] This movement is not Christian, as it denies that Jesus is the eternal God in flesh. It is also not scientific, believing that physical healing is a matter of the mind and prayer, mostly to the exclusion of medicine. William Kenyon and others accepted similar ideas in their understanding of Christianity in the twentieth century, influencing primarily Pentecostalism but also many other Christian traditions. Thus, the Word of Faith movement began in the 1960s, and its heresy lives on today through numerous Christian leaders around the world.[3]

Regrettably, the prosperity gospel rallies are often filled with poor people. Why? They believe in this false law of attraction, thinking that by being around these wealthy leaders, they too will become wealthy. They want what their guru has. They suppose, "If I have enough faith, I can drive the kind of car he does. I can live in the kind of home in which he lives. I can be as healthy as they appear to be."

Of course, members of the Word of Faith movement do not always agree with one another, but some extremists actually believe we can "speak" ourselves into becoming rich. I was watching television when one of these preachers said, "Just say, 'I am a millionaire.'" He wasn't satisfied with that and continued, "You need to proclaim, 'I am a billionaire,' and you can speak things into existence that aren't yet in existence." The power, according to him, was in your confession.

Throughout history, people have always attempted to manipulate "gods" to get what they want. The prophets of Baal in 1 Kings 18 cried out to their god, and when Baal appeared reluctant to respond, they cut themselves until their blood flowed, "after their custom" (v. 28). They even used this show of self-harm to demand an answer from their false god. But when Elijah prayed with a submissive disposition before the sovereign God Yahweh, he appealed to God's covenantal relationship with His people. God then answered according to His purposes. But we do not have the right to "put God to the test," insisting that He respond to our requests according to *our* will.

The God of Abraham, the Father of our Lord Jesus Christ, cannot be manipulated. When Jesus taught us to pray in Matthew 6, He began with worship and submission. Prayer is not about getting what we want, though God may graciously give it to us. Prayer is when we align with God's agenda, saying, "Your kingdom come. Your will be done." Of course, we present requests for provision, forgiveness, guidance, and daily bread. But we do not pray as the world does, heaping up "empty phrases" (Matthew 6:7). If we try to use the name of Jesus as a tool for getting whatever we want, we are not much better than the non-Christian exorcists in Ephesus who unsuccessfully used the names of Jesus and Paul to perform the miracles they had no right to perform (see Acts 19).

Prayer is not about getting what we want. . . . Prayer is when we align with God's agenda.

When we try to manipulate God, we often demand much from Him but nothing of ourselves. We pray, "God help me," but not "God forgive me." We might ask God for money but not the wisdom to spend our funds wisely. Prayer is more than asking—it is also obeying and thanking; it is committing and submitting. God is not a slot machine to get our needs met; He is a heavenly Father who seeks a relationship of submission and worship on our part.

However, there are some promises that can always be claimed! When Jesus said, "For God so loved the world, that he gave his only Son, that whoever believes in him should not perish but have eternal life" (John 3:16), such universal promises are given throughout the New Testament. If you are reading this and have never come to saving faith in Christ, do so right now! Jesus promised, "I am the resurrection and the life. Whoever believes in me, though he die, yet shall he live" (John 11:25). Such promises of salvation apply to everyone!

And for us as believers, we can always claim promises such as 1 John 1:9, that "if we confess our sins, he is faithful and just to forgive us our sins and to cleanse us from all unrighteousness." And we can always count on promises such as, "I will never leave you nor forsake you" (Hebrews 13:5). The list of such available promises is long and trustworthy.

God did not promise that we would be wealthy and healthy in this life. Forgiveness, *yes*; reconciliation with God, *yes*; the assurance of eternal life, *yes*! All that and more is available to all who are given the grace to accept it. But He never said we'd be rich and that we'd never suffer pain or illness.

This is a good time to pause and ask, what are some of the errors of the Word of Faith movement? Sometimes they use passages of Scripture, but do they use them correctly, in context, and in a way that is balanced? Let's discuss this in more detail.

Errors of the Word of Faith Movement

Here is a quick survey of a few of the errors in this movement.

Confusion Between the Old Testament and the New

It is easy to confuse the promises of prosperity in the Old Testament with the era of the New Testament. In the Old Testament, God dealt with Israel as a theocratic kingdom. As a theocracy, God had a covenant with the whole nation and ruled it directly by His law given at Sinai and the revelation given to the prophets. So, promises and curses were given to the people as a group, as a nation. In effect God said, "I am going to bless or curse you based upon your faithfulness to the law. If you follow me, I am going to give you riches and good crops. If you do not follow me, I am going to send you drought and grasshoppers." In other words, blessing was frequently defined in material terms. Possessions were often a sign of blessing (see Deuteronomy 28:2, 11).

So, the promises of earthly blessings were tied directly to the weather, to crops, and to livestock. But today we are under the new covenant based on "better promises" (Hebrews 8:6). Now the emphasis changes from material blessings to spiritual blessings; from obedience that produces wealth, to an obedience that almost always guarantees persecution. We are no longer a nation bound by physical boundaries, but a holy nation scattered around the globe, even among the poorest countries of the world.

Today, we are under a different arrangement. We do not have blessings and curses regarding crops based on whether we are faithful in keeping the Mosaic law. Under the new covenantal arrangement, faithful believers might be called on to suffer in many ways; some go hungry and are deprived of even the most basic necessities, like the apostle Paul experienced.

The new covenant that Jesus inaugurated before His crucifixion is now between God and all of us who believe in Him. We are far wealthier, spiritually speaking, than the saints of the Old Testament could have even imagined. We do not offer sacrifices because the perfect sacrifice has come. We do not just have a high priest who represents us; we are all priests and priestesses before God. And the list of blessings goes on and on.

We can ask for wealth and health in our era, but we cannot insist on it because we have no such guarantee or promise from God. And to all those preachers and teachers who tell us that we can claim health and wealth, I would rather that they look directly at their audiences and say, "It is more important for you to be holy than for you to be healed."

Ignoring the Necessary Conditions

Many of these Word of Faith preachers ignore some of the necessary conditions for answered prayer. If we read the New Testament uncritically, some of Jesus' statements seem as if they were blank checks, wherein we can simply fill in whatever we want. For example, Jesus gives some instructions to His disciples in the upper room, and His statement is often quoted: "Whatever you ask in my name, this I will do, that the Father may be glorified in the Son. If you ask me anything in my name, I will do it" (John 14:13–14).

Whatever we ask?

In context, Jesus is contrasting the old order with the changes that will take place after His ascension. He speaks of His followers doing greater works because "I go to the Father." The poured out Holy Spirit will give to the church an ability to proclaim the gospel with greater clarity after the resurrection and ascension. And of course, the worldwide church has proclaimed this gospel to multiplied millions.

Clearly, the name of Jesus is not a good luck charm that can be used to get whatever we want; this promise has to do with aligning ourselves with the glory of the Father and the will of His

Son. In the very next chapter, Jesus adds more clarification: "If you abide in me, and my words abide in you, ask whatever you wish" (John 15:7). In summary, we must be on His team and ask according to His game plan. There is nothing here to suggest that we can speak anything we want into existence.

Nowhere in the letters of Paul do such promises occur. Paul, for example, spoke about making our requests to God, but his specific promise is that "the peace of God, which surpasses all understanding, will guard your hearts and your minds in Christ Jesus" (Philippians 4:7; read vv. 4–7). He himself performed only one recorded miracle of healing and left his seven-year companion, Trophimus, sick (2 Timothy 4:20).

Yes, but Not Yet

There are many blessings Christ already purchased for us, but they are not available to us just now. Misled teachers tell us that a little more faith, a bigger declaration, and a heartfelt prayer are all that stands between us and the fulfillment of a promise of healing and wealth today.

Was physical healing in the atonement Christ purchased for us? Absolutely. Jesus died for us in entirety, including our bodies. The Bible says Jesus died to put away all sin. Sin is entangled with sickness, since sickness did not exist until after sin.

Isaiah 53:5 says, "But he was pierced for our transgressions; he was crushed for our iniquities; upon him was the chastisement that brought us peace, and with his wounds we are healed." While the text is predominantly about sin, it is also about physical healing. Jesus came and forgave sin, but He also performed healings to prove that the body was important. We are not just souls trapped in a body; in fact, the body is so important that someday it will be raised.

Since healing is secured and promised in the atonement, can we insist on healing whenever we want? Can we *demand* it from God because it is a part of our inheritance? Some people try! One time I heard a Word of Faith preacher say that words control the body. He preached that regardless of what's happening in a person's physical body, the person should actually speak to their major organs because the tongue controls the physical body. This preacher taught that we don't have to tolerate sickness and disease but instead speak the Word of God against them.

I heard another one say that if Jesus had not stopped talking on the cross, He would not have died; there is so much power in His words that the reason He died was because He quit speaking. (Sometimes, I fear that God's sheep cannot tell the difference between grass and AstroTurf!)

My parents knew a family who were wonderful Christians, but they believed healing was in the atonement, and because Jesus had provided it, we could have it all *now*. They said that they intended to not die but live until Christ returned. Moment by moment, they would claim the healing they believed was theirs, "by His stripes they would be continually healed." As they became sick, they aimed to constantly appropriate the work that Jesus did through the cross and the resurrection. A few years later, we received the news of their deaths. They could not reverse the inevitable effects of aging brought upon all of us because of sin. They would receive their healing when they arrived in heaven, but the day of resurrection is still future.

The good news is that our bodies will be healed—permanently. Our resurrection body was included in the work of the cross and the resurrection of Christ, but we do not inherit that today. We pray for the sick, but we cannot demand it and say, "You *must* heal me now," or "God is my healer, *today*."

No, God has not forsaken you! I understand that the challenges of life are overwhelming. But if you are hearing these false promises, please, my friend, recognize that these so-called Christian leaders are lying to you. The Bible says we are subject to the will of God, and that sometimes the will of God involves suffering just as it did with Jesus. Will you remember that Jesus' suffering led to glory? Your endurance today ultimately leads to great reward in the future. Do not give up! In fact, we must persist in prayer, seeking God for the strength to endure. We have all the resources we need to fight against Satan who wants us defeated. Let us, as Paul says, pray "at all times in the Spirit, with all prayer and supplication. To that end, keep alert with all perseverance" (Ephesians 6:18). Prayer frequently does not remove our trials but gives us grace to prevail in them.

A member of our church said his knee surgery was so painful "I will never have the other knee repaired until I am in the presence of Jesus." The good news is that in the presence of Jesus, he will get two brand new knees, hips that work, a perfect body, and a sharp mind. More than that, we shall receive a body, "like his glorious body" (Philippians 3:21). When we see Jesus, we shall be like Him for we shall see Him as He is. Until that time, sickness, heartache, and bad knees are unfortunately the norm. The waiting can seem cruel some days, when your body groans to rise from bed in the morning. But your perfect body is coming!

Should we stop asking for healing? No! Not at all. In the Old Testament, the promises of God showed that He was interested in healing. Jesus, of course, spent a good deal of His ministry healing all who came to Him, primarily to reveal Himself as the Messiah and Savior.

Yes, by all means, pray for healing!

I regard it as a travesty that so many Christians think immediately of their doctor more readily than they do of Christ when it comes to physical ailments. Certainly, God may use doctors, but why don't we seek God for wisdom when we encounter an illness? You can be sure that if I were told I had a terminal disease and under a doctor's care, I would still enlist others to pray for me. And, there are instances in which God graciously does heal the sick.

James 5:14–15 says,

> *Is anyone among you sick? Let him call for the elders of the church, and let them pray over him, anointing him with oil in the name of the Lord. And the prayer of faith will save the one who is sick, and the Lord will raise him up. And if he has committed sins, he will be forgiven.*

The very next verse speaks of confessing our sins one to another. In other words, we must always ask if there is sin in our lives blocking the answer to our prayers. At The Moody Church, we have anointed many people with oil when they came for healing, but we always met to counsel them first. I have even had a few instances where people testified that "a healing definitely took place." Praise God! Yet, James should not be misunderstood. The text does not say that everyone will be healed, regardless of the will of God.

In some instances, we anointed and prayed over a person with the elders, and God chose not to heal. Collectively, God did not grant us the "prayer of faith." Even though we were disappointed, we still praised God, because God also has a purpose in a lack of physical healing. In such instances, God wants to use our prayers to draw us closer to Himself and renew our faith.

Years ago, I encountered a very challenging situation. There was a wonderful group of students who belonged to a Christian organization committed to revival ministry. When their leader was diagnosed with cancer, I visited him and had an encouraging discussion about how he was approaching the end. I remember he said, "I want to believe in the dark what I have learned to trust in the light." Beautiful!

But there is more to the story. There was a godly revivalist who prayed much for this leader and concluded that God was going to heal him. This revivalist had such a sense of peace that he inspired others to expect healing. Well, to the surprise and disappointment of many, the leader died, but they didn't take his body away immediately in order to give God time for a resurrection. But, alas, that didn't happen.

How do we interpret this? I believe this revivalist interpreted the peace of God as the will of God as he understood it. As we seek God, He gives us peace, but that peace doesn't necessarily tell us what God is going to do; it does, however, prepare us for *whatever* God does.

To repeat my point: Let's be quick to ask for healing and even to hope for it, but we cannot *demand* answers in this life. Nor should we condemn those who pray for healing and God doesn't heal them. Imagine what happens when a person goes into a hospital room and tells the patient that he was sick because he didn't have enough faith. If he had more faith, God would heal him. Uttering words like this only lays a mountain of guilt on the patient. Another person told me about how people brought him books when he was in the hospital. But instead of encouraging him, the books were about healing, and the pages were highlighted with lines telling him that if he had faith he could walk out of the hospital. This "help" was no help at all.

The godliest people have all suffered physically and died. The martyrs of old who were killed for their faith come to mind—Stephen, Polycarp, and Perpetua. But, my friend, let not your heart be troubled, for death is not the end. Your inheritance—the *full* inheritance promised to you—is coming.

Later in this book, I will refer to Abraham, who saw only a glimpse of God's promises fulfilled. He received the fulfillment of the promise regarding a child—Isaac. But he didn't see the land of promise. And in a sense, Abraham is still waiting. The promises God made to Abraham have not been completely fulfilled to him and to his offspring. He died in faith believing in a city built by God (Hebrews 11:13). And we must do the same.

Our Limited Authority

Finally, many of these ministries fail to understand that our authority as believers is a limited, delegated authority. We do not have the same authority as Jesus. By faith, we are united *with* Jesus and we are *in* Jesus. But we are *not* Jesus. We cannot speak to storms and hurricanes like Jesus spoke to the raging Sea of Galilee and expect them to obey.

But again, some of the teachers of our time think we have almost unlimited authority. Kris Vallotton, one of the Bethel Church prophets of Redding, California, stated that "prayer is an act of leadership as it authorizes God to do His will on the earth."[4] Apparently, we are the gatekeepers, the authorizers of God's work in the world. He looks to us to see how He should act.

Years ago, a group of Word of Faith followers met in Washington, DC, to ban Satan from the city. They prayed to send him packing, barring him and his minions from entering the city again. They supposedly had that authority! But what do you think? Do you think God answered their prayer? I suspect that Satan is still active in our nation's capital.

If we could simply speak and pray with authority to banish Satan, we would banish him from the whole planet! If we ask why

God has Satan (or some other demons) in Washington, DC, the answer is, "Because the Lord has need of him." God uses Satan for His own purposes. And in the Scriptures, you won't find anything saying we have the authority to override or change God's decrees. God has given His people limited authority over the devil; we do have the authority to wage in victorious warfare against him. In fact, we should. But only God has *ultimate* authority.

When my co-writer Scott MacDonald moved to a new area, he was looking for a church to attend. One pastor he spoke with didn't hide anything and confessed that certain churches were preaching the prosperity gospel. "They make promises and people get disappointed when the promises do not come true." So, Scott asked him if some of those people had subsequently joined his church. He responded, "No. Once people are burned by the prosperity gospel churches, they want nothing to do with Christ." How easy it is to become disillusioned with Christ when the promises are misapplied!

One day I preached in a city where a Word of Faith preacher had promised that if people sent him money, their mortgage would be miraculously paid. I asked a pastor in the area what happened. He responded, "Hundreds of people sent that preacher money; no mortgages were miraculously paid. People are angry, turned off to Christianity." And though it's tragic, their response is understandable.

I've noticed that often the faith healer always comes out on top when his followers don't get what he promised them. If there's a miracle, he takes the credit; if there is no miracle, it's your fault because if only you had the faith, it would have happened. "Heads I win, tails you lose." That's gross abuse of power and influence.

These false teachers speak about blessings from God but not about brokenness before God; they speak of a crown without a cross and a vague belief in Christ without repentance. I have never seen or heard one lean into the camera and say, "It's better to be holy than healed!" Or, "It's better to seek righteousness rather than riches."

Of course, God is interested in all aspects of our lives—our present and our future. But we always have to remember that we are not in charge; all final decisions are His.

And yet He invites us to come and ask.

The Complexity of Prayer

Nothing I have said in the preceding pages should be interpreted to say that we should not bring all of our requests to the Lord and we should not bother to pursue Him. I must emphasize that we are invited to give Him no rest until we are satisfied that His will is done. Let me encourage you to seek God and His purposes.

Jesus told a parable about a widow who "kept coming to him" (a judge) and saying, "Give me justice against my adversary" (Luke 18:3); eventually, the judge became weary of her persistence and gave her what she requested. Then Jesus said, "And will not God give justice to his elect, who cry to him day and night? Will he delay long over them? I tell you, he will give justice to them speedily" (vv. 7–8).

Yes, Jesus began the parable by saying to His disciples, they "ought always to pray and not lose heart" (v. 1). Clearly, Jesus was saying that if we are not persistent in prayer, we will indeed lose heart. Let us determine that we will persist in our prayers especially where spiritual issues are at stake. My point in this chapter is that there are certain requests we cannot *demand* God to answer based on His promises. We must always be subject to His will and His purposes.

God does promise special blessings to those who will not give up on prayer, those who seek Him with their whole heart, whether they get all they ask for or not. If a worldly judge will respond to the prayer of a persistent widow, will not God hear the cry of His children?

Must we always end our prayer saying, "If it be Your will"? Later in this book, I will refer to some biblical prayers, which are exactly according to God's will. But when it comes to prayers that request a change of circumstances or to change other people to our liking, we must acknowledge that yes, God is the final arbiter. As we shall explain later, Jesus in the garden of Gethsemane requested not have to drink the cup given to Him, but then added, "'Nevertheless, not as I will, but as you will'" (Matthew 26:39).

Let us take comfort in the fact that God always hears us. Our prayers have reached His ears even if we do not get the response we desire. But in this book, we hope to give hope to those who ask and apparently do not receive, for those who are asked to go through some dark times without any improvement in their situation, be it ill health, poverty, loss, and their own death.

We pray that, through reading the pages that follow, your faith will be strengthened despite the unpredictability of God's purposes and the questions that inevitably arise because of seemingly unanswered prayers. Even as we are reminded that God honors persistence in our prayers, let us also resolve to keep trusting God even when we do not understand His ways.

Prayers You Can Be Sure God Will Answer!

The Bible makes it clear that God always responds to those who know they are sinners and come to Him in humility, seeking forgiveness and acceptance. God is willing and able to rescue us from the eternal consequences of our sins. Yes, there are some prayers God *always* answers!

Here are a few promises assuring us that everyone is invited to believe in Jesus for forgiveness of sin and the gift of eternal life—a journey with God in this life and then forever in the life to come. If you have doubts, bring those doubts to Jesus.

Hear this good news directly from Jesus:

> *"Truly, truly, I say to you, whoever hears my word and believes him [God the Father] who sent me has eternal life. He does not come into judgment, but has passed from death to life." (John 5:24)*

> *"But to all who did receive him, who believed in his name, he gave the right to become children of God." (John 1:12)*

> *"If you confess with your mouth that Jesus is Lord and believe in your heart that God raised him from the dead, you will be saved. For with the heart one believes and is justified, and with the mouth one confesses and is saved." (Romans 10:9–10)*

Do you wish to pray right now? The words are not as important as the desire of your heart, but here is a sample prayer:

> *"God, I know that I'm a sinner and stand in the need of Your forgiveness and grace. Right now, I am turning away from my sin to receive remission of my sins through Your Son, Jesus Christ our Lord, who died for me and was raised from the dead. I bring nothing to You except my great need, admitting my sinfulness and depending solely on Your undeserved grace toward me. Thank You for Your love for me. Amen!"*

A Prayer of Worship When We Want to Complain

Father,

We worship You today, even in our anger, frustration, and discouragement.

We confess that we have complained against You because life is often so difficult.

We have questioned Your ways, believing that if we had Your power, we could have done a better job of running this universe than You have.

Father,

We pray that we will not rebel against Your sovereignty.

When we see injustice in the world, may we not ascribe it to You.

May we remember that You, O Lord, are God, and we are not.

Help us to believe that Your way is perfect, even when we do not understand.

May our admission of this truth lead us to submission, repentance, and thanksgiving.

In Jesus' name, Amen.

When You Pray, "Lord *Help* Me! But Don't *Change* Me!"

Surrendering to God's priorities, not our own

Deceitful motives.

If you have lived in a city for any length of time, you have probably encountered people on the streets who are in need or experiencing homelessness. I have taken time to sit and talk and pray with many of them, and as I listened to them, I heard stories of family rejection, abuse, and substance addiction. Praise God that churches and ministries here in Chicago (and around the world) have been reaching out as the hands and feet of Jesus to care for and serve those in need of physical and spiritual help. At times, we may hesitate to help, wondering if money or other resources we offer will be misused. No one wants to help people hurt themselves.

Similarly, God's children can misuse the gifts He grants. Sometimes we pray to God with an entirely wrong motive, hoping for a financial windfall from Him, but then using what He gives us to fulfill selfish ends or getting frustrated when He does not give us what we want.

In this chapter, we'll confront the reality that many of our prayers are misguided, deceitful, and sinful. Perhaps God should say no to our prayers! But in the end, He doesn't turn us away; instead He wants us to pray with pure motives and lead us to Himself even as we come humbly into His presence. Sometimes He protects us by saying no.

Whether God says yes or no, one thing is sure: He intends for our prayers to change us. Many who pray, "Lord *help* me" should pray, "Lord *change* me!" God doesn't need changing, but we do. Personal transformation always lies at the heart of prayer regardless of how God answers.

When We Pray Deceitfully

Let's talk about the word *passions*. Some passions are good and biblical. We think of Paul's words, "Woe to me if I do not preach the gospel!" (1 Corinthians 9:16). We should have a passion to do God's will and fulfill our calling. Recently I heard the musician Michael W. Smith speak about having a passion for music as a ten-year-old. Scott, who is coauthoring this book, tells about his oldest son Malachi, who was enjoying reruns of the TV show *Little House on the Prairie,* which depicts Pa playing the fiddle. Around the same time, one of the women of his church was playing her violin in worship. Shortly afterward, Malachi declared, "I want to play a violin." Scott quickly seized upon that fruitful interest, and since then, Malachi has been learning to play. We might call that a "passion" to excel in music. I, personally, have always had a passion to preach the Scriptures.

But—and this is huge—we all know that we can have ungodly passions. Lust, pride, jealousy, and various forms of self-exaltation come immediately to mind along with a host of other sinful urges. James the Just, the half-brother of Jesus, writes to Christians who were ensnared by their passions and selfish desires. And in the middle of his incredibly practical instructions and rebukes, he talks about the issue of "asking" and "receiving"—a reference to prayer.

> *What causes quarrels and what causes fights among you? Is it not this, that your passions are at war within you? You desire and do not have, so you murder. You covet and cannot obtain, so you fight and quarrel. You do not have, because you do not ask. You ask and do not receive, because you ask wrongly, to spend it on your passions. You adulterous people! Do you not know that friendship with the world is enmity with God? Therefore whoever wishes to be a friend of the world makes himself an enemy of God. Or do you suppose it is to no purpose that the Scripture says, "He yearns jealously over the spirit that he has made to dwell in us"? But he gives more grace. Therefore it says, "God opposes the proud but gives grace to the humble." Submit yourselves therefore to God. Resist the devil, and he will flee from you. Draw near to God, and he will draw near to you. Cleanse your hands, you sinners, and purify your hearts, you double-minded. Be wretched and mourn and weep. Let your laughter be turned to mourning and your joy to gloom. Humble yourselves before the Lord, and he will exalt you. (James 4:1–10)*

Let's unpack this incredibly relevant passage.

Wisdom from Above and from Below

Back in chapter 3, James describes two different kinds of wisdom: wisdom from above and wisdom from below. The wisdom from above is "first pure, then peaceable, gentle, open to reason, full of mercy and good fruits, impartial and sincere" (v. 17). I think we all want homes and churches filled to the brim with wisdom from above.

However, James also describes a different kind of wisdom, which does not even deserve to be called wisdom. He labels this "wisdom" as "earthly, unspiritual, demonic" (James 3:15). It looks like bitter jealousy, selfish ambition, and disorder. We will call this the wisdom from below. And this contrast sets the context for James 4:1–10.

James is writing to people who see themselves as wise, but their wisdom is not from above, it's from below. These believers are characterized by disorder; they are quarreling and fighting among themselves. And these base passions lie behind their prayers or their lack thereof.

God rightly calls them "adulterous people," or literally "adulteresses" (4:4). These so-called Christians are like Israel in the Old Testament when they left their true husband (Yahweh) and whored after false gods, evil gain, and more (see Ezekiel 23).

So, these fleshly, earthly passions are no minor mistake. Their nature allies them with spiritual systems and unseen agents of evil. Evil starts in the heart, and when these desires are acted upon according to sinful nature, they are "friends of the world." And James points out that this has a direct bearing on their prayer life.

Wisdom from Below

When James speaks about "friendship with the world," he is not speaking about the physical globe or even the totality of humanity.

"World" in this text refers to the rebellious world systems. These are the systems and patterns of the age that teach people to "fight for what you want" and "seize your rights, even if hurts people." But the wisdom that comes from God says, "Love your neighbor" and "Why not rather suffer wrong?" (see Matthew 22:39 and 1 Corinthians 6:7). You see, when the people James was referring to quarreled, they were acting according to worldly priorities. They were conformed to the world and fit in beautifully with the mood and attitude of the ungodly around them.

James accuses them of being in cahoots with the devil. So, he writes, "You ask and do not receive, because you ask wrongly, to spend it on your passions. You adulterous people! Do you not know that friendship with the world is enmity with God? Therefore whoever wishes to be a friend of the world makes himself an enemy of God" (James 4:3–4). What a rebuke! Is it any wonder this path is described as demonic in James 3? When they follow their passions and ally with the world, they are on the devil's team. He is the father of their selfish quarrels. He is the coordinator of a world system of rebellion.

Sadly, this wisdom from below is not merely a plague upon the unconverted world; it's among God's people. It leads to quarreling and fighting. Nothing is quite as grievous as witnessing two brothers in Christ squabble over something, unable to resolve it between themselves. In today's society, such disputes are often played out on the internet in full view of the entire world. Online slander is sometimes justified as the need for transparency, and vengeance is often cloaked as justice. That's the wisdom from below.

James is telling them (and us) that they often don't pray ("you do not ask"), but when they do ask, they ask God for what they want rather than what He wants for them. If you have parented multiple children for any length of time, you know this problem. One child sees another playing with a toy. The child without the toy desires it in their heart. Instead of politely requesting a turn (or patiently waiting), the child acts upon their desire and provokes a confrontation to obtain it. Adults are not so different; we're simply more adept and cunning in fulfilling our covetous desires. And adults often expect God to be on their side of the argument.

James also says that economics plays a part in these arguments. Trade and commerce have caused some businessmen to plan as if they will always make a profit without a thought about the fact that they will die (see James 4:13–17). And how do they use their wealth? The short answer: for themselves, for their own benefit and desires. In fact, James had just rebuked them for praying for God's blessing that they will *spend* on their own desires (4:3). In the gospel of Mark, that word *spend* is used to describe the women with the bleeding disorder, as she had fruitlessly "spent" all her funds on doctors (Mark 5:26). But I find it especially appropriate how Jesus uses the word in Luke 15:14. When he describes the prodigal son who runs off into a far country, and he squanders and *spends* all his inheritance.

James is writing to recipients who are enthralled with gaining wealth to buy what the world sells: a fragile and temporary sense of power, pleasure, and security. And they are willing to fight each other for it. For the record, quarreling would not satisfy their desires. Quarreling and winning what they want would only further gratify and strengthen their evil passions. These immature and worldly Christians have tried this tactic: "I will just ask God for everything I desire." Why would God answer prayers like that?

In his short book *Prevailing Prayer*, D. L. Moody writes, "There are a great many prayers not answered because there is not the right motive; we have not complied with the Word of God; we ask amiss. It is a good thing that our prayers are not answered when we ask amiss."[1] God is not interested in giving His children everything they want. He is a better Father than that. He desires what is best for them and doesn't want His people to sink further and further into slavery to evil passions, friendship with the world system, and oppression by the enemy.

One more example. Jesus teaches on prayer in the Sermon on the Mount. Before sharing the Lord's Prayer as a model, He mentions the hypocrites in Matthew 6:5–6:

> *"And when you pray, you must not be like the hypocrites. For they love to stand and pray in the synagogues and at the street corners, that they may be seen by others. Truly, I say to you, they have received their reward. But when you pray, go into your room and shut the door and pray to your Father who is in secret. And your Father who sees in secret will reward you."*

Selfish passion is obviously at work. The prayer of the hypocrite is deceitful because he contorts its true purpose away from God to enrich himself with a worldly "reward." The hypocrite doesn't want God; he wants the world. The same could be said concerning those who "ask but do not receive" in James 4. In prayer, they desire something other than God. Avoid such deceitful prayers.

Because I read this passage recently in my personal devotions, I must refer to the prayer of the mother of James and John who ambitiously prays on behalf of her sons. You are acquainted with the story, but it deserves retelling:

> *Then the mother of the sons of Zebedee came up to him with her sons, and kneeling before him she asked him for something. And he said to her, "What do you want?" She said to him, "Say that these two sons of mine are to sit, one at your right hand*

and one at your left, in your kingdom." Jesus answered, "You do not know what you are asking. Are you able to drink the cup that I am to drink?" They said to him, "We are able." He said to them, "You will drink my cup, but to sit at my right hand and at my left is not mine to grant, but it is for those for whom it has been prepared by my Father." And when the ten heard it, they were indignant at the two brothers. (Matthew 20:20–24)

I have to say that in many ways, I love this mother. She boldly prays, face-to-face with our Lord. Parents always desire more for their child, and this request is for authority and greatness. Interestingly, Jesus does not exactly rebuke her but seizes this opportunity to teach that "whoever would be great among you must be your servant" (20:26).

Jesus would shortly demonstrate what it means to lead in the kingdom by suffering and dying at the hands of sinners to save sinners. Her prayer is deceitfully tinged with worldly ambition, seeking rulership for her sons, much as how the Gentiles ruled. People often pray for exaltation; however, as we will learn shortly, the path to exaltation lies in humbling oneself before God. Let us avoid such deceitful prayers.

Those who pray with wisdom from below use prayer like an oxygen mask on an airplane: glad He's there if needed but pay little or no attention to Him as long as life is going well. They expect God to do their will and refuse to bow humbly to His will. Tragically, God is used when needed, but He is not worshiped.

Wisdom from Above

Elsewhere in this book, I will emphasize praying the prayers of the apostle Paul, who always prayed "kingdom prayers" for spiritual growth and the exaltation of Christ. For now, I just want to ask:

Do you have a favorite prayer in the Bible? The pages of Scripture are filled with the prayers of God's people. Some are long, such as Jesus' prayer in John 17, which is the entirety of the chapter. Nehemiah 9 is mostly a substantial and humble prayer. First Kings 8 is predominantly King Solomon's magnificent prayer for the dedication of the temple. Meanwhile, short prayers are spoken with urgency (see Numbers 12:13 and Matthew 14:30).

Such prayers are prayed with "wisdom from above."

Sometimes in a desperate situation, we pray short prayers and God answers. A couple of years ago, Scott's wife, Michal, was riding to a Bible study. Her friend was driving. A newborn was in a car seat behind the ladies. The road was snowy, and as it turned out, it was icy. They hit a patch of ice and started sliding toward a deep ditch. But as they slid, Michal cried out, "Jesus, help us!" I think the Lord heard her in that moment as they descended into the ditch. When they came to stop, the women, the newborn, and even the vehicle were all perfectly fine. It was a short prayer of desperation and dependence, much like Peter when he shouted, "Lord, save me!"

If you want a good contrast between a prayer prayed with wisdom from below vs. a prayer prayed with wisdom from above, reread the parable of Jesus and notice the contrast; first the wisdom from below, and then the wisdom from above. He also told this parable to some who trusted in themselves that they were righteous, at the same time treating others with contempt:

> *"Two men went up into the temple to pray, one a Pharisee and the other a tax collector. The Pharisee, standing by himself, prayed thus: 'God, I thank you that I am not like other men, extortioners, unjust, adulterers, or even*

> *like this tax collector. I fast twice a week; I give tithes of all that I get.' But the tax collector, standing far off, would not even lift up his eyes to heaven, but beat his breast, saying, 'God, be merciful to me, a sinner!' I tell you, this man went down to his house justified, rather than the other. For everyone who exalts himself will be humbled, but the one who humbles himself will be exalted."* (Luke 18:10–14)

The Pharisee offers a deceitful prayer of thanksgiving, indirectly thanking himself for his righteous performance. It is really a prayer of pride and self-congratulation. We notice no awareness of his true condition.

But the prayer prayed with wisdom from above, that is a prayer from God's perspective. In this parable, it's the prayer of the tax collector who, in the presence of God, saw himself for what he was and begged for undeserved mercy. What a model for us when we pray!

I personally delight in corporate prayer, which is a balm to the soul. I rejoice knowing that right now, around the world, Christians are privately and corporately praying to the Father in the name of the Son by the power of the Holy Spirit. In persecuted countries, believers are gathering, praying for strength and guidance. In their great need, they have learned to pray with wisdom from above; they are praying not just for deliverance but for faithfulness whether deliverance comes or not.

As a pastor of The Moody Church, I attended and participated in the Wednesday prayer meeting each week when I was in town. I tried to always help us see beyond our present need and give thanks to God and worship Him. Yes, we made our needs known to God, but we always sought to combine those needs with thanksgiving and praise. And to be willing to submit to God's will. Only in this way can we know we're praying with wisdom from above.

So, what is James's remedy for praying with wisdom from above and not from below? He gave his listeners four commands to avoid the kinds of prayers God rejects; the prayers that are self-centered instead of Christ-centered.

Let's let these four commands revolutionize our often selfish prayer life.

Preparing Our Hearts to Approach God

James has diagnosed the problem of their fruitless prayer life and now instructs them on how to pray with a heart that seeks God. He points out that prayer is more than words.

Submit to God

"Therefore it says, 'God opposes the proud but gives grace to the humble.' Submit yourselves therefore to God" (James 4:6–7). If a word exists in our time that our culture hates more than "submit," I do not know of it. Personal agency is a cultural value. "Follow your dreams" is the zeitgeist. No one wants to submit. As long as you don't bother anyone, "you do you" is the standard.

However, to submit to God means that every one of our ambitions, every one of our dreams, has to be given over to Him, consciously and continually. We don't just pray a prayer of submission; we live a life of submission. All ultimate allegiance goes to the King of kings, even as we recognize that the head of the church is Christ, we still submit to our elders and leaders (Hebrews 13:17; 1 Peter 5:5). And, as appropriate, we submit "to one another" (Ephesians 5:21).

As Paul commands in Philippians 2:3–4, "Do nothing from

selfish ambition or conceit, but in humility count others more significant than yourselves. Let each of you look not only to his own interests, but also to the interests of others." In contrast to a world with its own agenda, Christians are people of submission—not a single Christian is exempt. The only reason we can submit in all these ways is because we first and foremost submit to God, rejecting the rule of our passions, the world system, and the devil.

Once we submit ourselves to God, our prayers are different. We sound less like a kid on Santa's lap reading a long Christmas list and more like Jesus in the garden of Gethsemane (more on that later). We turn from me-centered intercession to You-centered intercession. Instead of praying, "God, give us a home," we turn it into "God, provide for my family's need for housing in such a way that you are glorified and we have a witness in a community that needs you. We look to you and your will be done."

Once we submit ourselves to God, our prayers are different. . . . We turn from me-centered intercession to You-centered intercession.

Resist the Devil

James continues, "Resist the devil, and he will flee from you. Draw near to God, and he will draw near to you" (James 4:7–8). This is spiritual warfare; don't think that you can progress in your relationship with God without a fight from the devil. Every inch you move closer to God will be contested. Yes, I believe we have to pray "warfare prayers," putting on the full armor of God that we might be able to stand against the schemes of the devil. This deserves more attention than I can give it here, but no one can be a conqueror without being able to resist satanic opposition.

Resist all the excuses for your prayerlessness. The devil will attempt to put a dozen ideas in our minds as to why we should not pray: lack of time, fruitlessness of results, the enticing videos on YouTube, or the evil one tells us that God doesn't really care, etc. Resist and stand in the victory of Christ!

Whether you feel like it or not, pray with an attitude of complete submission to God! And yes, you do have time to pray!

Purify Your Heart

James then continues with these words, "Cleanse your hands, you sinners, and purify your hearts, you double-minded. Be wretched and mourn and weep. Let your laughter be turned to mourning and your joy to gloom" (James 4:8–9). What a description of repentance! Let God search our hearts and reveal all of our sin so we can confess it and forsake it and find mercy.

Again, our age inculcates the opposite. The posts on social media endlessly affirm us, saying, "You are perfect just the way you are." Even the urge to promote a healthy lifestyle and encourage people to take care of their body can be labeled as "body shaming." Various kinds of desire, even sexual practices once seen as vices, are protected as an inherent aspect of the self. "It is just the way you are." Then the affirmation follows, "You should accept yourself."

We live in constant struggle. In Galatians, Paul says "the desires of the flesh are against the Spirit, and the desires of the Spirit are against the flesh" (read Galatians 5:16–26). As James 4:8 says, we are "double-minded." Our hearts are duplicitous, and we feel the tension. Instead of following our flesh with its strife, rage, dissension, envy, drunkenness, and sensuality, we must purify ourselves from such evil. We crucify the flesh. We kill it. How? We must "walk by the Spirit," bringing forth the fruit of the Spirit with love, joy, peace, self-control, and more.

We all know people who are struggling with their flesh, and we have all been there. We must take drastic action, separating ourselves from the paths leading us to repeat the deeds of the flesh. We must learn to walk daily by the power of the Holy Spirit. And when you choose to love your neighbors—and even your enemies—you will have no room in your life for rage (or other evil desires of the heart)!

The internet, with all of the good that has come of it will, nevertheless, tempt us to impurity, to jealousy, to unneeded curiosity, and every form of sensuality.

Yes, it is a struggle, and I hope you seek accountability from a mature believer in your church. But when God directs you to purify yourself, it is not hopeless. When the Scripture commands you to cleanse yourself "from every defilement of body and spirit, bringing holiness to completion in the fear of God" (2 Corinthians 7:1), God is not setting you up for failure. Your heart and your hands can be holy in Jesus Christ.

God does not affirm you (or me). We are sinners; He is a holy and righteous God who cannot affirm us as we are. He can, however, redeem us—as we are, right at this moment. He loves us and He changes us, transforming us into the image of His Son. And by His Spirit, we are not passive in the metamorphosis. We are commanded to actively participate in the transforming, purifying work of God. And in this pursuit, our prayers change too. In fact, our prayers will begin to pursue greater and greater transformation. Instead of desiring more and more stuff, we will increasingly plead for more and more holiness.

"I cried to him with my mouth, and high praise was on my tongue. *If I had cherished iniquity in my heart, the Lord would not have listened*" (Psalm 66:17–18). James would shout to us across the centuries, "Purify your hearts!"

Humble Yourself

A friend of mine has pointed out that humility is not a fruit of the Spirit; humility is something we are asked to do, involving choices we make with God's help. Don't overlook both this rebuke and this promise, "Humble yourselves before the Lord, and he will exalt you" (James 4:10). Have you noticed the world exalts the proud and overlooks the humble? God does the opposite: He exalts the humble and rebukes the proud.

Here in Chicago, the city has an annual Pride Parade. People are openly proud of shameful acts. We see pride in other ways too. For example, maybe you have heard someone say, "I needed to get a divorce because I needed to finally do something for me." Their friends pat them on the back and say, "Good for you," while giving no thought concerning the virtue of marital fidelity, the destruction of a home, the pain of a spouse, or the confusion of a child. Pride can manifest in even more subtle ways. Many people will proudly declare, "Look what I have made of my life," yet give no credit to the God who gives "life and breath and everything" (Acts 17:25).

In prayer, a proud heart demands from God, believing He owes us. "We have worked so hard, God. We are blessing so many people. Look at all the people coming to faith through us. Surely, you must grant us this request. What more could we do?" We have all fallen into this sin.

In prayer (often paired with fasting), a humble heart asks with no expectation other than God's glory and will. Thinking little of themselves and much of God, humble believers present their requests without supposing that God is obligated to give them whatever they ask. Why? They know they don't deserve anything, and so anything God provides is an act of grace—of unmerited favor.

James wrote, "God opposes the proud but gives grace to the humble" (4:6). Let us pray that we may submit, purify, and humble ourselves so we can pray rightly and receive God's grace. And in this way, God will gain a victory in our lives, even if some specific requests go unanswered.

Right now, dare to draw near. Obey the words of James, "Draw near to God, and he will draw near to you" (v. 8). Come into God's presence, not to change Him but rather to be changed by Him. Let all excuses be put aside and let your only agenda be to seek His agenda. Stripped of pretense, weary of self-exaltation, tired of repeated sin—come!

A Prayer for Purity and Humility

Are we ready to pray for purity? We are content to pray for stuff, for healing, and the like, but we are slow to pray for purity. We are cowards in prayer. We might say we want revival in our lives, but we want it our way, conveniently and painlessly. Then we pray soft prayers, with whole areas of our lives untouched by penitence, submission, and confession. Our lives remain impure.

Why do we pray so tentatively? Like a dying man fearfully pushing away a life-saving surgeon, we do not trust the One who holds the knife—the One who grasps our life—to do the best for us. We have no faith, and we are resigned to our spiritual sickness. Seeking purity starts by praying that the Surgeon gets His way in our lives.

Hold nothing back.

Lord,

Purify me in entirety—any means necessary.

Do what You must; spare no part of me.

I trust You. I choose to trust You.

I confess that I have feared Your work, thinking that maybe You would change me too drastically.

I surrender. Discard what You must;
tear away whatever You will.

God, I beg You to push me to pray with
abandon, that I may stop trying to
save my life and instead lose it.

I want a faith in which I am satisfied by You alone,

Wherein I demand no comforts,

Wherein I expect no part of my
life to remain untouched.

Forgive me for my callous and proud heart.

I have avoided prayers of radical transformation.

I have been content with a Christianity
that never changed me,

Performing a masquerade of piety,

Wallowing in spiritual mediocrity,

Pursuing the earthly before the heavenly,

Praying for "strength" and "healing" while
failing to ask for purity and humility.

I admit my self-deception, trying to
hide my sin from You and others.

In prayer, I acted as if I did not need you.

Among others, I proudly displayed
my self-righteousness.

Honesty begins with me today.

I have been a coward in prayer.

Lord, have mercy on me.

Do whatever you must in my life to purify me.
Do whatever it takes for me to pray with humility.

Come what may.

In Jesus' name, Amen.

When the Answer Is *Yes* but Not What You Expected

When God answers the prayer of our hearts not the words of our lips

Hospitality comes in different forms.

Back in college, supper was the social hour. If we wanted to have a conversation with someone, we made plans to arrive at the cafeteria at the same time. We would sit together and discuss the events of the day. Eating and talking together was how many of us forged deep connections and had life-changing revelations. I suspect you and I might even still be friends with someone with whom we regularly shared a work lunch.

Did you know Abraham had a working dinner with God? Yes, you heard me correctly. It took him a while to realize whom he had invited into his tent. It was just a normal, uneventful day when three men randomly showed up, and according to ancient Near Eastern custom, he had the responsibility of taking care of them. Little did he know who they were or how their visit would put into motion a need for desperate prayer.

Let's visualize the scene.

Abraham is sitting in the shade at the door of his tent when three men arrive. Instinctively, he seemed to know that these three men were not ordinary bedouins. He not only bowed before them but called one of them "Lord" and despite his one hundred years, he acted swiftly. "And Abraham went quickly into the tent to Sarah and said, 'Quick! Three seahs (about five gallons) of fine flour! Knead it, and make cakes.' And Abraham ran to the herd and took a calf, tender and good, and gave it to a young man, who prepared it quickly" (Genesis 18:6–7). That is a lot of food, all done in a hurry.

The three men gather under a tree, and a few hours later, Abraham feeds them the best he possibly can.

Who are these three men? As it turns out, one of them is the Son of God. He has not yet been born to Mary and He has not yet been named Jesus. Yet He occasionally appeared in the Old Testament as "the angel of the Lord." In the New Testament, we read that even the prophet Isaiah saw Jesus' glory during his temple vision and spoke of Him (see John 12:37–41). The point is this: God has never been far from His people. Here in Genesis 18, one of three men is called the "LORD," meaning Yahweh, so, we can reasonably conclude He is the pre-incarnate Son of God and the other two are angels.

This meeting is alluded to in Hebrews 13:2, where it says, "Do not neglect to show hospitality to strangers, for thereby some have entertained angels unawares." Abraham does well to show hospitality to his heavenly guests.

The Conversation Begins

While Abraham and his guests are eating, the guests speak. "Where is Sarah your wife?" Wait a moment! How do they know her name is Sarah? Abraham answers and says, "She is in the tent." The Lord answers, "I will surely return to you about this time next year, and Sarah your wife shall have a son" (Genesis 18:10). Again, who speaks like this? Only the Lord!

The text continues, "And Sarah was listening at the tent door behind him. Now Abraham and Sarah were old, advanced in years. The way of women had ceased to be with Sarah. So Sarah laughed to herself, saying, 'After I am worn out, and my lord is old, shall I have pleasure?'" (Genesis 18:10–12). With obvious biological impossibilities, Sarah's laughter seems like a plausible response to the Lord's declaration.

But Sarah's laugh is a chuckle of disbelief. In the previous chapter, God spoke with Abraham predicting that Sarah would bear a son (see Genesis 17:15–21); yet apparently, Sarah had not believed the news. Abraham appears to believe, but Sarah does not. She is not loud; she is laughing to herself. Yet she is overheard, and the Lord responds:

> *The LORD said to Abraham, "Why did Sarah laugh and say, 'Shall I indeed bear a child, now that I am old?' Is anything too hard for the Lord? At the appointed time I will return to you, about this time next year, and Sarah shall have a son." But Sarah denied it, saying, "I did not laugh," for she was afraid. He said, "No, but you did laugh." (Genesis 18:13–15)*

God is reminding Sarah that a miracle is possible. He can take a nearly one-hundred-year-old man and a ninety-year-old woman and give them a son. It's not too difficult for God. Sarah gets caught both in disbelief and in a lie. Not a great day for Sarah (though I am sure the bread cakes were fantastic).

Nothing is big to God. He is all-present and all-powerful. Sometimes when we pray, we say, "Now Lord, I am just praying about something small." But even if we are praying about something big (to us), it is all small to Him. Hurricanes are like a ripple in the pond. Planets are but bouncing marbles, and the regions of outer space like the dimensions of our back yard.

Nothing is too difficult for the Lord.

One-on-One with God

After the meal was over, the three men begin to go toward the city of Sodom. Two of the men—the angels—move off, and Abraham stands alone in the presence of the Lord. As we read the text, we are allowed to enter a divine soliloquy. The Lord of glory is talking to Himself, and He speaks within Abraham's hearing:

> *"Shall I hide from Abraham what I am about to do, seeing that Abraham shall surely become a great and mighty nation, and all the nations of the earth shall be blessed in him? For I have chosen him, that he may command his children and his household after him to keep the way of the LORD by doing righteousness and justice, so that the LORD may bring to Abraham what he has promised him. . . . Because the outcry against Sodom and Gomorrah is great and their sin is very grave, I will go down to see whether they have done altogether according to the outcry that has come to me. And if not, I will know." So the men turned from there and went toward Sodom, but Abraham still stood before the Lord.* (Genesis 18:17–22)

You must read this with some theological glasses. The Son of God is not on a reconnaissance mission trying to find out the state of Sodom and Gomorrah. Put this paragraph in the same category as God asking Adam in the garden, "Where are you?" God knew where Adam was. And God knows the state of Sodom. But here God is presenting Himself as a human being, and so He speaks in anthropic (human) language. God talks like one of us. And in saying that He is going to check out how bad Sodom has become, Abraham realizes that Sodom faces imminent judgment.

Abraham boldly instigates and intercedes. His nephew, Lot, and Lot's family are living near Sodom (see Genesis 13). Abraham could not stay silent. He speaks with a trembling voice:

> *Then Abraham drew near and said, "Will you indeed sweep away the righteous with the wicked? Suppose there are fifty righteous within the city. Will you then sweep away the place and not spare it for the fifty righteous who are in it? Far be it from you to do such a thing, to put the righteous to death with the wicked, so that the righteous fare as the wicked! Far be that from you! Shall not the Judge of all the earth do what is just?" And the LORD said, "If I find at Sodom fifty righteous in the city, I will spare the whole place for their sake." (Genesis 18:23–26)*

Oh, to be a bystander watching this play out! Abraham's knees are quaking. He realizes that he's in the presence of God who can make the decision whether Sodom will be destroyed. Abraham knows Lot lives there, the nephew he rescued in Genesis 14. You might recall that after Abraham rescued him, Lot went back to Sodom. Abraham is thinking of Lot, his wife, and their daughters, and so he daringly negotiates with God. The starting number? *Fifty righteous people.*

Abraham began rather high. Sodom and the surrounding cities of Gomorrah, Zeboiim, Admah, and Zoar were not exactly a hotbed of righteousness. But how does Abraham attempt to negotiate? He appeals to the justice of God. An interesting choice. Abraham was not going to defend the unrighteous people of Sodom. He knew they didn't deserve mercy. Instead, Abraham focuses on the hypothetical righteous people of Sodom. Yes, Sodom deserved punishment, but would it not be unfair to have some righteous people get swept away in the destruction? And while judgmentthroughout history often include the unrighteous and the righteous, God agrees to relent of His wrathful designs if fifty righteous people are in Sodom.

But Abraham is nervous as he reflects on how wicked Sodom is. So, he begins to take advantage of the moment and negotiate downward, lower and lower until he ends with just ten righteous people.

The intercession continues and we can just feel the tension:

> *Abraham answered and said, "Behold, I have undertaken to speak to the Lord, I who am but dust and ashes. Suppose five of the fifty righteous are lacking. Will you destroy the whole city for lack of five?" And he said, "I will not destroy it if I find forty-five there." Again he spoke to him and said, "Suppose forty are found there." He answered, "For the sake of forty I will not do it." Then he said, "Oh let not the Lord be angry, and I will speak. Suppose thirty are found there." He answered, "I will not do it, if I find thirty there." He said, "Behold, I have undertaken to speak to the Lord. Suppose twenty are found there." He answered, "For the sake of twenty I will not destroy it." Then he said, "Oh let not the Lord be angry, and I will speak again but this once. Suppose ten are found there." He answered, "For the sake of ten I will not destroy it." And the*

LORD went his way, when he had finished speaking to Abraham, and Abraham returned to his place. (Genesis 18:27–33)

What about forty-five? What about forty? What about thirty? Twenty? Ten?! It probably feels quite impertinent and presumptuous to speak with God in this way, and that is why Abraham employs statements like, "Let not the Lord be angry" and "I am but dust and ashes." Yet God loves Abraham.

To be clear, Abraham was not really bargaining with God, and nor should we. When you bargain with someone, you have something to give in exchange, or you are haggling over a price. Abraham arrives at this conversation empty-handed. He brings nothing to the table except his concern for Lot and for God's righteousness. That is all that he has. He pleads, and God answers out of His kindness. Then the Son of God leaves.

What do you think Abraham told Sarah that night in the tent? I cannot prove it, but I suspect he said, "Sarah, I just talked God out of destroying Sodom." I can imagine Sarah responding, "Oh, Abe, that's wonderful! You and God have got this thing going." Then they maybe do a little bit of math. Abraham ponders, "Let us double check. Ten righteous people. Yes, yes. Lot is down there. He has his wife and his two daughters." That is four. Sarah chimes in, "And don't forget that the girls are about to be married, and those two men must come from four good parents." Abraham sighs in relief, "So four in Lot's family plus six makes ten!" He sleeps well thinking he had saved Sodom from judgment. Today, we'd say that Abraham deserves the "World's Greatest Uncle" coffee mug.

The next morning Abraham is shocked. He can't believe what his eyes are telling him.

And Abraham went early in the morning to the place where he had stood before the LORD. And he looked down toward

> *Sodom and Gomorrah and toward all the land of the valley, and he looked and, behold, the smoke of the land went up like the smoke of a furnace. So it was that, when God destroyed the cities of the valley, God remembered Abraham and sent Lot out of the midst of the overthrow when he overthrew the cities in which Lot had lived. (Genesis 19:27–29)*

I doubt Abraham thought God had lied to him. Instead, he probably realized, "Wow, there were not even ten righteous people in Sodom. I wonder what has become of Lot." The answer to that question is not plain to Abraham, but the next chapter tells us the story and it isn't pretty.

After a shocking scene of attempted sexual violence (both homosexual and heterosexual), the two angels rescue Lot, his wife, and two daughters. Just four people were saved from the fire. And, disobeying clear instructions as they escaped, Lot's wife looked back at the city and was turned into a pillar of salt. Only three people escaped the fire and brimstone. And what happened next with these three in a cave is a story of deception and incest.

But let's leave the story there and ponder what this teaches us about intercession, prayer, and the lessons this story gives us.

Prayer and the Providence and Purposes of God

In passing, we should note that God could have destroyed Sodom and Gomorrah, including Lot and his family, without breaking faith with Abraham. Simply put, there were not ten righteous in Sodom. Abraham overestimated the number of righteous, so if Lot and his family had died in Sodom, God's promise to Abraham would have remained unbroken.

In the end, Abraham's intercession did not affect God's plan to heap fire and brimstone on Sodom and the surrounding area. God agreed with every number Abraham suggested. Why? God knew full well that the number of righteous people in the city was too few. Judgment was inevitable.

Abraham had his prayer answered, but not in the way he expected. God saw past Abraham's words and looked directly into his heart. His prayer was answered in a way he never dreamed. *He would not get what he had prayed for, but he did get what he had hoped for.*

Let's pause and ask what this teaches us about intercession, requests, and answers.

Friendship and Fellowship Lead Us to God

Reading this story, I can't help but think that the closer our friendship with God, the more freely He shows His intentions with us. We sometimes hurry over accounts like this far too quickly. God comes with two angels to eat at the table of Abraham who's sitting under a tree. What an awe-provoking event! The Divine Sovereign of the universe comes from heaven and meets a tent-dweller.

Why does Abraham get a special visit?

Abraham was a "friend" of God (see James 2:23, Isaiah 41:8, and 2 Chronicles 20:7). That title "friend" is used uniquely of Abraham in the Bible, though friendship with God is not limited to him (see Exodus 33:11 and John 15:15). Brothers and sisters, if we are friends of God, He is more disposed to share His intentions with us. In this way, He helps us pray.

But listen to this and be blessed.

Jesus said to His disciples, "No longer do I call you servants, for the servant does not know what his master is doing; *but I have called you friends, for all that I have heard from my Father I have made known to you.* You did not choose me, but I chose you and appointed you that you should go and bear fruit and that your fruit should abide" (John 15:15–16). Imagine! We stand on the same ground as Abraham; we too can plead for our families!

The nearer we are to God and the more we abide with Him in friendship, the more He discloses to us. And He enables us to pray differently because we begin to discern His mind and His heart.

God doesn't meet with us as He did with Abraham, but I have experienced—and I'm sure you have also—that God gives us a burden to pray for people or certain situations because He intends to bring about His purposes, and we're a part of the ends to which He is working. As we learned in the previous chapter, "Draw near to God, and he will draw near to you" (James 4:8).

Let's make the most of our friendship with Jesus!

Don't turn away from Him when you need comfort; come to Him with any request, then trust Him for the results. It might not be exactly what you prayed for, but it might be what your heart longs for. The first purpose of prayer is fellowship and intimacy with God, and we repeatedly must return to "the God of all comfort" in our disappointments. *When the answer to a request means more to us than God Himself, we are missing the primary purpose of prayer.*

Before anything else, the purpose of prayer is to develop friendship. And when this pursuit is first, we become satisfied even if we don't get what we think a good God should give us. We see an amazing example of that fellowship as God eats with Abraham under a tree. And today, Jesus says to us, "Behold, I stand at the door and knock. If anyone hears my voice and opens the door, I will come in to him and eat with him, and he with me" (Revelation 3:20). In prayer, He still reaches out to us, drawing us into friendship with Him.

I cannot state this too strongly: You will become quickly disappointed with prayer if you presume that its first purpose is getting what you need or want. The first purpose of prayer is for us to come before the Lord, yielding in faith and learning to enjoy fellowship with God. Whether He gives us what we ask for or not, it doesn't shake us. It only deepens us in our desire to know Him better. If you live like that, you will be at a prayer meeting. Do not let the pressing matters of intercession supplant the blessed fellowship of prayer.

In the fourth century, Athanasius of Alexandria wrote a description of a remarkable man of prayer, Anthony of the Desert. Anthony's parents died when he was young, and he dedicated himself to the Lord's work. He gave much to the poor and lived for decades in the Egyptian desert. But first and foremost, Anthony was a man who dwelt with God. He instructed others, "Pray continually; avoid vainglory [pride]; sing psalms before sleep and on awaking; hold in your heart the commandment of Scripture."[1]

You will become quickly disappointed with prayer if you presume that its first purpose is getting what you need or want.

Like Abraham, he walked with God. We can too.

Be Prepared for a Surprising Answer

Let me repeat: God denied Abraham his request, but He still gave him what he wanted. Abraham's concern was for Lot and his family, and I doubt it dawned on Abraham that there might be more than one way to spare his nephew and his family. When God says no to a request, the answer could be denied or delayed or answered in a different way. God evacuated Lot and his family out of Sodom before destroying the city.

We also experience God working differently than we expect. Have you ever noticed how often we are wrong when we think we know how God is going to act? God seldom answers in the way we think; He is so creative. He balances many more concerns than one alone. He is wise and insightful, confounding our small minds. If we have a preconceived idea of how God should answer, we might miss seeing His answer altogether.

Abraham would have continued to walk with God even if Lot and his family had been destroyed in Sodom. God had every right to sweep Lot away with the entire city. God is waiting for us to set aside our prayer list and prioritize spending time with Him in quietness, meditation, and submission, listening to His voice through His Word. *We might not have our request answered, but we do have God!*

The Bible has other examples of these "different" answers. At the end of King David's life, he said in effect, "Lord, I would love to build a house for you. I want to build a temple. I have the time, the money, and the organization. I am readying the materials. Let me build you a house" (see 2 Samuel 7). That prayer sounds like an automatic *yes*. Of course, God should approve David's plan! Yet God responds, "David, the answer is *no*. But I am going to build *you* a house." That was a surprise. God doesn't want David to build Him a house, but God wants to build David a house (a lineage through which the Messiah would be born). By God's design, David's house lasts forever. The very stream of history is shaped around David's offspring, for Jesus, the King of kings, came from David's lineage.

But God was not done with David's request. Even though David was not allowed to build the temple, God permitted David to collect the materials so that David's son Solomon could build it. God essentially said, "David, even though your motives are right and you want to build the temple for My glory, I want you to know that the desire of your heart is going to be fulfilled. But Solomon will do it, not you." David's request was honored, the temple would be built, but not by him. His son would become the answer to his request. David likely did not expect that answer.

A Few Righteous Can Have a Mighty Impact

The impact of the righteous is greater than their numbers would suggest. If ten righteous people had been in Sodom, God would not have destroyed it. This whole world is under the judgment and condemnation of God, and yet God withholds judgment because in every country of the world there are believers who love and serve Him. The few hold back the judgment for the many.

The world undervalues Christians. We are seen as obnoxious, and unfortunately, sometimes we are. We are seen as those who impede progress. We are painted by the media as people who want to impose our values. We are often misrepresented. But we are of great value in blessing the nations. Jesus said concerning His followers, "You are the light of the world. You are the salt of the earth" (see Matthew 5:13–16). As we preach the gospel, live godly lives, honor government, promote education, and help the poor, we preserve society from total decay. And in this way, we may actually stave off the judgment of God.

Temporal judgments are one thing; eternal judgments are quite another. The final decision regarding judgment is in the hands of Jesus: "Fear not, I am the first and the last, and the living one. I died, and behold I am alive forevermore, and I have the keys of Death and Hades" (Revelation 1:17–18). Thanks to Christ, those who trust Him cannot be swept away together in eternity with the ungodly. Jesus always has the final word.

Finally, let me remind you one more time that just as Abraham drew near to God and interceded for Sodom, you and I can also draw near to God and intercede for those around us. Abraham did not have some special privilege we lack. We have the privilege of entering the "the holy of holies," the very presence of God. We get to stand where Abraham stood.

The privilege to draw near is ours in Christ. We are invited into the throne room of the King of kings. Here is a promise we should claim regularly: "Therefore, brothers, since we have confidence to enter the holy places by the blood of Jesus, by the new and living way that he opened for us through the curtain, that is, through his flesh, and since we have a great priest over the house of God, let us draw near with a true heart in full assurance of faith" (Hebrews 10:19–22).

Come with confidence to intercede for your family, your church, your city, and the nations of the world. Expect God to answer according to your prayers but also look for unexpected answers. If He doesn't answer according to your expectations, remember that you have that which is most important: fellowship with a God who loves you and who you love even though we can never fully understand His ways. Our responsibility is fellowship and worship; His responsibility is to answer according to His will.

A Prayer to See Things God's Way

Are you frustrated with unanswered prayer? I (Scott) have been there, praying and praying for a fellow believer to get well. Then she died. Did my prayers mean nothing to God? I thought we were friends!

But as I grieved, I came to realize that I was not dealing with unanswered prayer—not at all. I was blind to God's answer since He answered in a way that was different from my expectations. I prayed for healing, and in a way, God gave it. My friend is more alive now in heaven than ever before, and the resurrection is still yet to come.

God,

One more prayer,

One more time.

Here and now,

Hear my crime.

I pray for answers, not for You.

I am blind to Your purposes because

I only see my own plans.

Permit my foolishness no longer.

Change my heart, clear my eyes,
direct my gaze, lead my steps.

I want to walk with You.

One more prayer,

Not for me, but for You.

Here and now,

Let our friendship renew.

In Jesus' name, Amen.

When a Prayer for Peace Ends in a National Disaster

But if you have a pulse, you still have a praise!

"Where is God?"

We have all asked that question when we see the injustice in the world, when gangs rule the streets and the poor are ravaged. When corruption prevails in the courts, and honesty is nowhere to be found, we wonder if God still sees it all, and if He does, how He puts up with it. When the righteous are marginalized and the powerful increase in wickedness, we wonder how God's people can interpret it. When the wicked prosper without rebuke, where is God?

A prophet in the Old Testament faced this question. He was as puzzled as we are, begging for an explanation of God's apparent silence in the midst of increased violence.

Habakkuk is called a *minor* prophet, but of course, the moniker is not to minimize his message. It simply means he wrote a short book, especially compared to the giant volumes of Jeremiah, Isaiah, and Ezekiel. But as the prophet cries out, "Where is God?" these three chapters speak to us in a big way about our relationship with God and God's relationship to us. Habakkuk gives us helpful insight when our prayers are unanswered.

Habakkuk had a privilege you and I don't. We can describe his interaction with God as a phone call: He spoke and God answered; he spoke again and God answered. And so it went. The book displays this back-and-forth dialogue he had with the Almighty. As we read his book, it's as if we've been dropped into the middle of the prophet's prayer closet.

The Earnest Prayer

Let us begin with Habakkuk's first prayer in chapter 1.

> *O LORD, how long shall I cry for help, and you will not hear? Or cry to you "Violence!" and you will not save? Why do you make me see iniquity, and why do you idly look at wrong? Destruction and violence are before me; strife and contention arise. So the law is paralyzed, and justice never goes forth. For the wicked surround the righteous; so justice goes forth perverted. (Habakkuk 1:2–4)*

Habakkuk is essentially saying, "I am praying to you, God, but where are you? How can you look upon this wickedness and do nothing?" We can see his frustration, grief, and tears seeping through the page.

He has two problems with God. First, God appears to be *deaf*. "LORD, how long shall I cry for help, and you will not hear?" (v. 2). The pagans shouted more loudly as they pleaded with their idols to listen to their cries. Habakkuk is beginning to wonder if he has to do that since God doesn't seem to be listening. And, quite honestly, all of us have felt that way at times when the heavens appear silent.

Habakkuk also is thinking that God must be *blind*. "Why do you make me see iniquity?" (v. 3). He's saying, "I see rampant iniquity all around me, but apparently You don't!" Elsewhere in the Old Testament, God leveled this charge against the idols of the nations. But here, Habakkuk throws it back on God because it appears God is unresponsive.

Thanks, but This Isn't the Answer I Wanted to Hear

After Habakkuk's initial prayer of complaint, God responds, provoking deep perplexity in the prophet. He wasn't expecting this.

> *"Look among the nations, and see; wonder and be astounded. For I am doing a work in your days that you would not believe if told. For behold, I am raising up the Chaldeans, that bitter and hasty nation, who march through the breadth of the earth, to seize dwellings not their own. They are dreaded and fearsome; their justice and dignity go forth from themselves. Their horses are swifter than leopards, more fierce than the evening wolves; their horsemen press proudly on. Their horsemen come from afar; they fly like an eagle swift to devour. They all come for violence, all their faces forward. They gather captives like sand. At kings they scoff, and at rulers they*

> *laugh. They laugh at every fortress, for they pile up earth and take it. Then they sweep by like the wind and go on, guilty men, whose own might is their god!"* (Habakkuk 1:5–11)

Stunning.

God is doing something! But what He's doing shakes the prophet to the core. "Habakkuk, you don't think I'm doing anything? I am. I am raising up an exceptionally evil nation by the name of the Chaldeans (more commonly known as the Babylonians), and I'm doing something you wouldn't believe. The Babylonians are coming to ravage your land."

This news from God is shocking, and God is allowing Habakkuk to feel its full impact. God is saying, "If you think Judah has problems now, look out because it's going to get worse. Today's difficulty is going to become tomorrow's disaster." God is saying He is neither deaf nor blind. What He's doing is invisible to the human eye, but eventually, it will become known—and it won't be pretty. Tough times are going to become tragic times.

The prophet didn't receive the answer he had hoped for. If you continue reading the text, you could imagine Habakkuk saying, "After that answer, I'm sorry I asked. I could have lived without this answer."

Many of us pray and lament to God on behalf of the United States of America (and many other countries). We cry to God: "God, the nations and their rulers belong to You. You raised up this nation. Please bring righteousness to our homes. Please bring justice and peace to our society and remove wickedness. Please help us!" But God's answer is often unpredictable. He may send revival, or He may send judgment. Of course, we know that God dealt with Israel in a way that He does not deal with countries today this side of the cross. His judgment of that ancient nation was often corporate and immediate; and usually it was delivered as defeat on the battlefield. But what we learn from this prophet applies: God often does not answer the requests we make for our families or our country, but rather brings us a very unexpected response. And, yes, things might get worse rather than better. We can be sure that continued rebellion in a nation will bring accelerating moral and spiritual decline. And even though God gives His people grace to live above the cultural decay, we still experience suffering from an imploding culture. Yet, He gives us the grace to remain faithful to Him, no matter the future. We have much to learn from this prophet and his prayers.

As Habakkuk did, we, at times, might wonder if we have read God's will correctly. His response is not what we were praying for. We pray for blessing; He answers with hardship. Sometimes He sends mercy; at other times, He sends judgment.

Struggling with God's Justice

Habakkuk wonders how this news of the coming Chaldeans could possibly be consistent with the God he thinks he knows. So, he continues to dialogue with God.

> *"Are you not from everlasting, O LORD my God, my Holy One? We shall not die. O LORD, you have ordained them as a judgment, and you, O Rock, have established them for reproof. You who are of purer eyes than to see evil and cannot look at wrong, why do you idly look at traitors and remain silent when the wicked swallows up the man more righteous than he?"* (Habakkuk 1:12–13)

The prophet knows God's attributes. The problem is that he can't square God's attributes with God's answer to his prayer with what he sees in the world. We can identify. We say, "God is love." Oh, really? If God is love, why would He not protect a young child from starvation and war? That scenario (and many others) is the struggle of every human being who has believed in God. We fail at our attempt to harmonize God's attributes with what we encounter in the world.

So, Habakkuk tells God, "O LORD you have ordained them as a judgment, and you, O Rock, have established them for reproof" (v. 12). The prophet acknowledges that the Babylonians deserve judgment. They were cruel, evil pagans who should be justly punished for their deeds. Sure, the Israelites are bad, but not *that* bad. So, Habakkuk continues, "You who are of purer eyes than to see evil and cannot look at wrong, why do you idly look at traitors and remain silent when the wicked swallows up the man more righteous than he?" (v. 13).

Yes! Traitors do often swallow up the righteous!

To Habakkuk, God's coming judgment is worse than the original problem. He again accuses God of being idle toward the plight of God's people. Of course, Habakkuk would admit that the people of Judah were evil. He already says that justice is absent and violence is present in the land. The commands of God are not being followed. But! To paraphrase Habakkuk's response: "We are *not* as bad as the Babylonians. Yes, Judah is evil as a nation, but the Babylonians are a 'bitter and hasty nation,' 'dreaded and fearsome,' filled with 'violence' and 'guilty men.'"

What about America? We, like Habakkuk, might think we are better than a lot of other nations: "Yeah, America has its problems, but surely, we are not *that* bad." We admit we are debunking moral sanity in favor of rampant individualism where truth is whatever an individual thinks it is, but we do not officially condone acts such as killing someone who converts from one religion to another.

So, we complain about how God judges us along with more wicked nations that are clearly eviler than we are. We would agree with Habakkuk, sending worse people to invade Judah because of its sin seems inconsistent with His justice and holiness. How can He stand and watch this? "You are of purer eyes than to see evil!"

The Posture of the Prophet

But Habakkuk's perplexity does not lead to the deconstruction of his faith; he has not given up on God. He assumes a posture. In chapter 2 he says, "I will take my stand at my watchpost and station myself on the tower, and look out to see what he will say to me, and what I will answer concerning my complaint" (Habakkuk 2:1).

We visualize him on a rampart. He is looking into the distance to see if any enemy is coming toward the city. Perhaps he was expecting an invading army bringing immediate judgment, but he also wanted to be the first to see God's response. Instead of Habakkuk's perplexity morphing into anxiety or anger, he stands in reverence, waiting on the Lord and His response.

And God does respond.

> *"Write the vision; make it plain on tablets, so he may run who reads it. For still the vision awaits its appointed time; it hastens to the end—it will not lie. If it seems slow, wait for it; it will surely come; it will not delay. Behold, his soul is puffed up; it is not upright within him, but the righteous shall live by his faith." (Habakkuk 2:2–4)*

So, that was God's initial response. Habakkuk waited. He heard. He wrote down God's answer. And as we read, we are transported to that rampart with the prophet. We stand and listen with him.

Did you notice a very famous verse? "The righteous shall live by faith." Three times it appears in the New Testament (Romans 1:17; Galatians 3:11; Hebrews 10:38). We've already referred to it in a previous chapter. The righteous shall live by faith; but what kind of faith is this? We know it's faith in God, but faith for what? As we look around us today, times are hard for many people. Economic instability persists. People are enduring sickness and poverty, and our nation lingers in a desperate state, morally and spiritually. What should we have faith in God for? God's answer to Habakkuk explains what we should believe and what our faith should accomplish.

First, God assures Habakkuk that judgment is coming to the wicked; the Babylonians will not be exempt from judgment. God gives five woes (or curses) in answer to Habakkuk's prayer and question. God will judge the Babylonians, but first He will use them to punish Israel.

> *"Woe to him who heaps up what is not his own."* (2:6)
>
> *"Woe to him who gets evil gain for his house, to set his nest on high, to be safe from the reach of harm!"* (2:9)
>
> *"Woe to him who builds a town with blood and founds a city on iniquity!"* (2:12)
>
> *"Woe to him who makes his neighbors drink."* (2:15)
>
> *"Woe to him who says to a wooden thing, 'Awake.'"* (2:19)

God recognizes the wickedness of the Babylonians and curses them. Through this, God reminds Habakkuk that He is a good judge. Yes, the Babylonians are a violent people, and they would bring terrible violence and death to Judah. But wicked people of every kind, of any religion, of any country, including Judah, never escape God's meticulous judgment. The standard of God's judgment and holiness had not changed one iota.

God says He will judge them "at the time appointed." We want justice today, but God is willing to wait until tomorrow. God tells Habakkuk and us, "I have my own timetable." In Ecclesiastes we read, "Because the sentence against an evil deed is not executed speedily, the heart of the children of man is fully set to do evil" (Ecclesiastes 8:11). People think, "I'm not getting caught. I made my money (through unrighteous means), and I have not been punished. My friends do the same, and they have gotten by. Everybody is doing it, and God is doing nothing."

In essence, God tells Habakkuk, "You don't have to see what I am doing, just know that I am working behind the scenes; My holiness and justice will be honored. I know exactly what is happening, and judgment will come." Despite the difficulties of Judah's present and future, Habakkuk could trust God's sovereignty and judgment. The "just shall live by faith." Habakkuk didn't see it and neither have we, but God promises that "the earth will be filled with the knowledge of the glory of the LORD" (Habakkuk 2:14). The Lord is supreme and holy, and someday soon, His glory will fill the earth.

Earlier in the first chapter, Habakkuk complained about how God was apparently silent in the face of a world filled with evil. Now, he reverses his mindset and says, "The LORD is in his holy temple; let all the earth keep silence before him" (v. 20). Habakkuk decides it is his turn to be silent.

As a matter of fact, the entire world should remember that God is in His temple; and in His presence, our mouths must be closed. We might not understand His ways, but it is all under His control. And ultimately, Earth will be filled with His glory!

A Prayer That Began with Perplexity Ends with Praise

Unanswered prayer. Unanswered questions. But despite his initial disappointment, Habakkuk now bursts into a hymn of trust and praise. Why? He has heard from God who has all things under His control! So, an unanswered prayer resulted in undiluted praise. Habakkuk's prayer is life-changing, from asking to worshiping.

If you read the next few pages with an open mind, inviting the Holy Spirit to bless and encourage you, they could be life-changing.

Habakkuk's prayer comes in two parts; he rehearses the *past* faithfulness of God, and then he tells us how he will face the terrifying *future* that awaits him.

First, he recalls what God has done, contemplating the works of God and the splendor of the heavens: "His brightness was like the light; rays flashed from his hand" (Habakkuk 3:4). The prophet continues, "Before him went pestilence, and plague followed at his heels" (v. 5). God even scattered mountains! Habakkuk is employing wonderful hyperbole throughout this section to portray the power of God.

Most commentators believe that he is alluding to the deliverance of the children of Israel from Egypt. As the text goes on, it talks about the seas, the rivers opening, and the pestilence that came upon Egypt. Habakkuk is lost in wonder as he looks at the past and begins to reminisce concerning God's accomplishments.

Take time to read it, and remember there is more to follow:

> *O* LORD, *I have heard the report of you, and your work, O* LORD *do I fear. In the midst of the years revive it; in the midst of the years make it known; in wrath remember mercy. God came from Teman, and the Holy One from Mount Paran. His splendor covered the heavens, and the earth was full of his praise. His brightness was like the light; rays flashed from his hand; and there he veiled his power. Before him went pestilence, and plague followed at his heels. He stood and measured the earth; he looked and shook the nations; then the eternal mountains were scattered; the everlasting hills sank low. His were the everlasting ways. (Habakkuk 3:2–6)*

And now we come to the second part of the prayer; he is applying the admonition to his uncertain future. The greatness and faithfulness of God in the past, now motivates him to pray a prayer we should pray as we face our own uncertain future.

Please read carefully and prayerfully:

> *I hear, and my body trembles; my lips quiver at the sound; rottenness enters into my bones; my legs tremble beneath me. Yet I will quietly wait for the day of trouble to come upon people who invade us. Though the fig tree should not blossom, nor fruit be on the vines, the produce of the olive fail and the fields yield no food, the flock be cut off from the fold and there be no herd in the stalls, yet I will rejoice in the* LORD; *I will take joy in the God of my salvation.* GOD, *the Lord, is my strength; he makes my feet like the deer's; he makes me tread on my high places. To the choirmaster: with stringed instruments. (Habakkuk 3:16–19)*

He concludes with this unbelievable, almost surprising burst of praise. And the prophet finishes with a note for the choirmaster. Why? This is a song. The people of God sang it!

Notice the realism of his fear and the answer of faith. The prophet is afraid. He trembles and quivers. Yet despite his fear and his frustration, he remains patient; he is willing to wait and let God act on His agenda on His schedule.

Do we not feel the same fear when things go bad in our lives? When we read tragic headlines, we wonder what will become of us! But justice is coming. We can wait rather than take vengeance or succumb to bitterness. "Beloved, never avenge yourselves, but leave it to the wrath of God, for it is written, 'Vengeance is mine, I will repay, says the Lord'" (Romans 12:19). Let us fear God, trust Him, and wait.

Let's now make this prayer our own for our moment of uncertainty!

The Prophet Still Had a Pulse, So, He Still Had a Praise!

How did Habakkuk move from *perplexity* to *praise* and from *worry* to *worship*? He was strengthened by two attributes of God we all know but so often do not rely upon. These are attributes in which we can trust when life becomes hard and every worldly thing you relied upon is gone.

First, God is in *control.* The Babylonians are coming! That is scary. They are wicked and evil. They skin people alive. They're renowned for their violence. God says, "I'm the one raising up the Babylonians, that bitter and hasty nation that shall come against you. That is part of my work as a discipline and as a judgment for your sin. But I am in control."

Have you ever wondered how strong the Babylonians were? Have you ever wondered how strong radical Islam is? Have you ever wondered how much authority Pilate had over Jesus? Have you ever wondered how strong the devil is? If you are thinking, "Yeah, I would like to know," keep reading.

How much power do the devil and wicked people have? *As much as God lets them have and not one whit more.* Satan cannot even harass you unless it passes Jesus Christ's test of control. For example, the devil wanted Peter, but Jesus said, "Simon, Simon, behold, Satan demanded to have you, that he might sift you like wheat, but I have prayed for you that your faith may not fail. And when you have turned again, strengthen your brothers" (Luke 22:31–32). Jesus is asserting that Satan cannot get to Peter unless the Lord permits it. Peter's situation was well in hand; the devil was subject to the purposes of Jesus.

Once we understand the limitation of Satan and the control of God, we pray with great faith because we know that God has everything under His command. We should remember Jesus' words to Pilate—words I absolutely love: "You would have no authority over me at all unless it had been given you from above" (John 19:11). All power ultimately belongs to God, and He gives it out as He chooses.

Evil people may harass you. You may endure great injustice. Your life circumstances may feel out of control. People may marginalize and misunderstand you. But remember this: Evil can have no authority over you unless it is given from above. That is why we pray to God, and that is why we have times of prayer and fasting. We must submit everything to God; we can come to God about anything because He is in control.

Habakkuk realized that nothing was happening by chance among the nations. God stands behind everything. He doesn't do evil but uses it for His own purposes. Yet through secondary causes, God is involved in everything that transpires on His planet. God is in control. That is the first truth of Habakkuk that leads to his song of worship.

Second, when Habakkuk recalls the story of the Israelites and their deliverance out of Egypt, he remembered something else about God. He remembered the *care* of God. He thought of how God led them through the Red Sea, how God held back the water, how God fed them, how the mountains trembled, and how God delivered His people by His sovereign hand. The prophet realized, "I believe that God *cares* about me." And in this way, Habakkuk chose to stop interpreting the silence of God as the indifference of God.

Habakkuk chose to stop interpreting the silence of God as the indifference of God.

Sometimes, God is silent, but that doesn't mean He's inactive. God may be silent, but the very hairs of your head are still numbered. You may be unable to see what He is doing, but He still sees the sparrow fall to the ground. You, a child of God, are still number one on His list of things to take care of in the universe. The prophet leads us to say, "I will accept the fact that sometimes God is silent. But He is faithful. *I don't have to see what God is doing in order to know that He is active. He sees and He cares.*

If Habakkuk spoke to us today, he might say it this way:

> *Though the refrigerator is empty, though I may lose my job and my livelihood, though life may turn against me, though what I plan may not come to pass, or I might be told I have a terminal*

disease, yet I will rejoice in the Lord my God. I will take joy in the God of my salvation, for the Lord God is my strength, and I will go on believing and trusting, no matter what.

When God puts us through the furnace, the fires of difficulty, He keeps His hand on the thermostat. We are assured that nothing is happening randomly, nor beyond His direction and interest. For God, all things work toward their appointed ends.

How Habakkuk's Prayer Motivated a Man Struggling with Depression

William Cowper (1731–1800) struggled with what we might call severe mental illness and attempted suicide on several occasions. He was the man who gave us the wonderful line that "God moves in a mysterious way, his wonders to perform." He also wrote the hymn, "There is a fountain filled with blood drawn from Immanuel's veins, and sinners plunged beneath that flood lose all their guilty stains."

Some people are saved, yet they struggle with mental illness, depression, and a sense of hopelessness. No matter our individual struggle, every child of God needs the church. Not one of us can live the Christian life successfully on our own. We all need to get to know other believers and pray with them. We need to become part of a body that helps us in our walk with God. One of us could be a Cowper, looking for help. One of us could be a John Newton, Cowper's dear friend, pastor, and counselor.[1]

Cowper wrote a hymn based on his personal interpretation of Habakkuk's prayer. One of the verses of "Sometimes a Light Surprises" reads:

Though vine, nor fig tree neither
Their wonted fruit should bear;
Though all the fields should wither
Nor flocks nor herds be there;
Yet God the same abiding,
His praise shall tune my voice,
For, while in Him confiding,
I cannot but rejoice.[2]

In Cowper's trial, despite his nearly lifelong depression, he placed his trust in God. Like Habakkuk, he somehow found joy in the control and care of God. God does not have to answer your prayers in order for you to rejoice in Him. If you are willing to trust God's control and care, your life can change today. Circumstances might not change but your heart will.

If we understand the meaning of the word *commit,* we will not find ourselves praying the same prayers over and over again. We leave those matters with God, and our prayers will turn to times of praise whether our prayers are answered or not. I find it very comforting that God uses imperfect people—people who struggle, people who go from hope to despair. I find myself having to repeatedly commit matters to the Lord because anxiety steals back into our hearts very easily. But I've discovered a great deal of difference between "praying" about something and truly "committing" something to God. Commitment means we take the matter from our shoulders and transfer it unto the One about whom the Bible says, "the government shall be upon his shoulder" (Isaiah 9:6).

I recently talked to a man struggling with anxiety because of his circumstances. He believes that he will not be able to earn enough money for his family; of course, part of his answer is to do all he can to find a job. Prayer is never a justification for laziness. But like all of us, he has to commit the matter to God for wisdom, guidance, and the next step. To do that, he has to know that God cares. Years ago, a young medical student met with me and said, "I am so full of anxiety. I can't even sleep because I think I might flunk out of medical school."

Let's not minimize these burdens. But Jesus taught us that anxiety doesn't have the ultimate power; so, I urged this medical student to do what I've had to do multiple times, say: "God, You are fully in charge. I will do the best I can, but this is Yours and not mine." His response was, "I can't do that, because if I do, God might let me fail medical school anyway." True. Committing your burden to God doesn't mean you'll pass medical school, it only means you'll accept it and move on to see what God has for you in the next chapter of your life.

We pray, pray, and pray. But do we trust? Praise and adoration will begin to displace worry and anxiety. Then, like Habakkuk, you can say, "Even though the worst time should come, I will still rejoice in God." However, you cannot arrive at that joy by just praying. You can only get it by that transfer of trust to God.

Take an hour (at minimum) and be alone with God. Set down the book you're reading; turn off Netflix, your smartphone, or computer; and spend some time before God with your face to the floor in silence. Then say, "God, I cannot bear these burdens. You never intended me to. I am going to agree with You about everything and completely commit my life and my future to You."

Expect a struggle. Your flesh, even a demon, might whisper, "Yeah, but what if God doesn't come through?" Stay in prayer as long as you need to. Persist until you leave your anxiety in God's hands. And in the end, you should be able to say, "Even if the fig tree does not blossom, even if the crop fails, even if my mental or physical illness isn't healed, even if there is not enough money, even if the relationship doesn't work out, I will still rejoice in God because it is not my burden. It is His."

Recall. "Humble yourselves, therefore, under the mighty hand of God so that at the proper time he may exalt you, casting all your anxieties on him, because he cares for you" (1 Peter 5:6–7). Humble yourself and cast your anxiety upon God. Now. Not later.

There's an old story about a woman carrying a heavy burden. She was so relieved when she was able to board a bus. Yet she stood in the middle aisle, continuing to lift the heavy suitcase. A fellow passenger said, "Put it down." She said, "I'm glad the bus is carrying me. I cannot expect it to carry my suitcase too."

If you are a believer, you are on the bus. Put your burden down. God's answer to your prayers might be perplexing, but of this we can be sure: *Our perplexity is intended to lead to praise.*

Yes, as someone told me, "If you have a pulse, you still have a praise!"

A Prayer of Remembrance

I (Scott) have yet to see one of my children wake up in the morning and greet me with a befuddled, "Who are you?" They remember me. They know my character. From their childlike point of view, they can recall some of the highlights of my provision for them. They can tell of family adventures in the Rockies. They can speak about the countless times they've gone to the grocery store. They even can talk about how their dad helped kill a cobra in their kitchen in Zambia. (They really like telling that story!)

Sometimes children have a better memory than most adult Christians. Too often, we forget our closest relation—our Father God. We let His works pass from our thoughts. We are like the wicked who forget God, whom God threatens to tear apart in Psalm 50:22. We are children who are served by a Father each day, even as we forget His face and treat His voice as unrecognizable.

Lord, have mercy on us, and grant us a remembrance of Your care and control.

God of our salvation,

We confess our flagrant forgetfulness.

We forget Your past works, Your past provisions, Your past patience.

Acting as if You have done nothing, we remain ever skeptical toward Your care for us today.

Overcome by anxiety and discouragement, we blurt out blasphemies,

"God does not see.

God does not act.

God does not care."

*Out loud or in our thoughts, these
contemptuous lines are uttered,*

By our ignorant actions,

By our half-hearted prayers,

By our godless attitudes.

Renew our faith.

You do see—even though we do not.

You do act—on your better timetable.

You do care—somehow more than we do.

*We commit our difficulties, our
trials, our anxieties to You.*

*Though our life is in disarray, though our future is
uncertain, though our death is near,
we remember Your faithful works, and we
rejoice in You, the God of our salvation.*

In Jesus' name, Amen.

When the Request Is Denied

When God substitutes one gift for another

Unanswered prayer may take many forms.

A little girl prayed that the doll in her arms would become a real baby, and when that Pinocchio-style wish did not come true, she was done with God. I know a teenager who prayed that his teeth would be straightened out so that he would not have to wear braces. And when his prayer was not answered, he asked, "Why bother with this business of prayer?" There are those who say God answers all of our prayers; it is just that He answers some by saying no. But that isn't very comforting, is it? The fact is, a no is still a no.

That being said, unanswered prayers are never wasted. There are purposes, sometimes clear, sometimes hidden but always intended to draw us toward God and not push us away from Him.

The great apostle Paul also tells us of an earnest prayer of his that went unanswered; but in his case, he was given special revelation to peer behind the curtain and see that God was using his disappointment as a stepping stone to greater things.

Although a no is a no, behind the scenes, there is more to the story.

Paul's Story

The apostle Paul was caught up to the third heaven in a vision. "Heaven" is a flexible term and can refer to the sky or space. But when the Scripture mentions the "third heaven," it's a reference to the highest heaven. We are talking about the seat of God's rule over all His creation. God is everywhere, but His presence is also localized. Paul was caught up to this heavenly paradise where God gave him specific revelations. Paul's questions were answered; those answers help us understand our own unanswered questions as well.

If Paul were like people today, he'd be on podcasts talking about this "vision." But Paul was wiser than many of the preachers of today; we live in an era when people are often quick to tell you about any vision they experienced. But Paul waited fourteen years before he spoke of it, and when he finally told his story, it was with a great deal of restraint.

> *I know that this man was caught up into paradise—whether in the body or out of the body I do not know, God knows—and he heard things that cannot be told, which man may not utter. On behalf of this man I will boast, but on my own behalf I will not boast, except of my weaknesses—though if I should wish to boast, I would not be a fool, for I would be speaking the truth; but I refrain from it, so that no one may think more of me than he sees in me or hears from me.* (2 Corinthians 12:3–6)

Who is the man that Paul knows? The apostle knows him very well, since he is talking about himself in the opening verses. Yes, fourteen years beforehand, Paul had been caught up to the third heaven. He has no idea exactly how it happened—in the body or not. But he knows that it happened. He heard things that cannot be told, which a man may not utter. So, he kept all the details under wraps.

The apostle Paul had many revelations. The Spirit worked uniquely through him as an apostle of Christ. Under the direction of the Spirit, Paul wrote thirteen or fourteen books of the New Testament (depending on who you think authored Hebrews). Either way, Paul wrote a good part of the New Testament. But with all of these revelations, Paul was concerned that if he told people this vision and they knew the wonders revealed to him, they would give him too much honor. Then he would be susceptible to thinking he was special, that he was worthy of such honor. Pride could pounce upon Paul and ravage the fledgling churches that looked to him for direction. Not only that, but he didn't want others thinking they should expect a similar experience.

Paul wrote that to prevent him from becoming prideful, he was given a thorn in his flesh, a messenger of the devil to harass him:

> *Three times I pleaded with the Lord about this, that it should leave me. But he said to me, "My grace is sufficient for you, for my power is made perfect in weakness." Therefore I will boast all the more gladly of my weaknesses, so that the power of Christ may rest upon me. For the sake of Christ, then, I am content with weaknesses, insults, hardships, persecutions, and calamities. For when I am weak, then I am strong. (2 Corinthians 12:8–10)*

What Was the Thorn in the Flesh?

The Greek word for "thorn" is *skolops*; it evokes a stake upon which people were impaled. It was a horrendous way to die. Because the word conjures up that image, many people think the thorn was a physical ailment. Some think it was an eye problem because he mentions signing his name in large letters (see Galatians 6:11). Perhaps Paul did have problems with his eyes. Or perhaps it was malaria, which can cause debilitating headaches. According to sufferers, it's like someone has pressed a hot iron bar against their forehead. Or perhaps the thorn is more spiritual. John MacArthur goes to great lengths to argue that the thorn in the flesh was probably a false apostle indwelt by a messenger of Satan (a demon) who stirred up opposition against Paul.[1]

Paul's vagueness allows us to insert our own thorn into this slot: a health problem, a handicap, or a painful special need. Or our thorn may be a person (I hope it is not the person you married!), but we all have experienced people who are like a thorn in our flesh, causing misery and difficulty. Paul gives us a lot of latitude. He says, "I am content with weaknesses, insults, hardships, persecutions, and calamities." You can probably find your thorn somewhere on that list.

I do not normally allow the church to vote on a biblical interpretation. But one day, when preaching on this text at The Moody Church, I asked, "How many of you would say that the thorn was from Satan? Raise your hands." I saw a sea of hands. Then I polled the church once more. "How many of you would say that the thorn was from God? Raise your hands." Even more hands shot up for that option. Then I asked the most important question. "How many of you raised your hand twice, saying that it was *both* from Satan and from God? Could I see your hands, please?" The wise few who raised their hands were correct. Yes, it is *both*!

The *immediate* cause of Paul's difficulty was a messenger of Satan, but the *ultimate* cause was God. Paul says that the thorn was given to him by God, but God used Satan to bring it about. The same is true of Job's trial. It is Satan who killed his children and cattle. The devil did all these terrible things; yet Job, being a good theologian said, "The LORD gave, and the LORD has taken away; blessed be the name of the LORD" (Job 1:21). The ultimate cause is God. Satan cannot wiggle an inch unless God gives him permission. Job's and Paul's trials were ultimately from God.

The Characteristics of Paul's Prayer

Let us look at Paul's prayer itself. He summarizes, "Three times I pleaded with the Lord about this, that it should leave me" (2 Corinthians 12:8). What do we say about this request?

First, it was *specific*. We may think Paul prayed something like this, "Father, You have given this issue (e.g., person, health issue, etc.) to me, Lord. I ask that You might remove it from me for Your glory, and I promise You will get the credit. I and others will talk about You and honor You. You will receive the glory. Help me, Lord."

Paul probably sounded like that because the prayer was specific.

Paul was also *persistent*. "I pleaded with the Lord." The New Testament also uses that word, "pleaded," to describe people who came to Jesus wanting to be healed. They pleaded; Paul pleaded.

The first two times, God said nothing. Paul found himself speaking to a silent heaven. Then after Paul prays a third time, God granted him a reply. The message was easy to summarize: No.

Paul kept the thorn, but that was not the end of the story. God didn't leave Paul stranded. God says, "My grace is sufficient for you, for my power is made perfect in weakness" (v. 9).

Imagine the conversation. Paul hears, "Paul, I have something else for you. I have grace." Paul then thinks, "Surely, there is a misunderstanding. I prayed very clearly that my thorn was to leave." But God says, "Keep your thorn, but accept special grace." God's grace is enough. Grace is heavenly strength for the need of the moment. Grace is a river that runs to the soul bringing inner healing, calmness, acceptance, hope, and even gladness. God's grace given to Paul is like salve on the thorn. God supplies exactly what Paul needed to endure the trial.

Grace is a wonderful pillow upon which many a weary traveler has laid his head. Receive it. Expect physical healing or deliverance from your situation; but if that doesn't happen, embrace God's grace. You can weather any journey with it. God's power is made perfect in Paul's weakness. If we want to honor God and give Him glory, we must be weak. The thorn accomplishes that mission, ensuring Paul's weakness and humility. And through it all, God's grace and power is displayed.

When God says no, that is not the end of the story. It is always, "No, but I have something else in mind."

When I was growing up on the farm many years ago, we used a print catalog to order things; that was the only way to do so. Many of you only know of online catalogs. If we ordered a blue sweater and the store was out of blue sweaters, they might send you a green one of the same size, hoping you'd be satisfied with the substitution. They usually didn't say, "We will not fill the order." They filled it with a substitute. God is saying to the apostle Paul, "I am saying no to your request, but I am making a substitution. I am not indifferent to your request." When God says no, that is not the end of the story. It is always, "No, but I have something else in mind."

God said to Paul, "I will not give you the gift of healing, but I will give you the gift of my grace."

I have often mentioned Joni Eareckson Tada. She has blessed millions through her testimony and her ministry. We hosted her at The Moody Church many times. Because of her diving accident decades ago, she became a quadriplegic. She wanted to die. She hoped and begged that people would give her pills so she could commit suicide and get out of her misery. Praise God, nobody did, and she went on living. Then, at the encouragement of friends, she attended faith healing services with the hope of being healed. She was encouraged to read John 5. In that story, Jesus healed the paralytic by the pool of Bethesda. He had been there for thirty-eight years, and Jesus came along and said, "Take up your mat and walk." Joni dedicated herself to that passage, but even though she thought she had faith, even though she believed God could and did heal, the healing never came.

Forty years later, with a worldwide ministry, she told how she was taken to Israel and wheeled next to the pool of Bethesda in Jerusalem. I remember listening to her with tears in my eyes as she said, "When I looked at that pool, I thanked God that He had not healed me forty years ago because of all the grace and ministry He gave me as a result of my infirmity." Just like Paul, God said, "Joni, I am not going to heal you, but I am not going to just abandon you there hopelessly. I am not indifferent. I am going to give you grace."

I know a family who lived with a disabled child; this girl is far beyond having a normal disability, and these parents lovingly care for their child with exasperation because they watch their child suffer every day. They have the best medical care, but nothing can be done for the suffering. And as you parents know, you suffer with your child when they suffer. Honestly, I confess that I do not have the grace to look after a child such as that, but listen carefully: If God had given me a child like that, I believe that He would have supplied grace or healing. But He would never leave me and my wife helpless. God gives grace in the midst of our need. God often says no to our requests for healing, but it is not a harsh or uncaring no. There is some higher purpose He has in mind.

Paul requested. God replied. What is Paul's response? "Therefore I will boast all the more gladly of my weaknesses, so that the power of Christ may rest upon me" (v. 9). He recognizes that if he receives God's grace, he also receives God's power. Paul prayed to get rid of the thorn, but thanks to God's grace, he has come to terms with his daily predicament. Both grace and power would carry him through. Paul is at peace with it.

Theologically speaking, we need to think carefully here. The thorn was described as a messenger (literally, "angel") of Satan. This thorn had its origins in the demonic realm. Whether a demon was directly present or not, we cannot determine from the text. But if Paul lived today, some preachers would have told him: "You need to bind and banish that demon. Your suffering can end today because you have authority over all evil spirits." No, that is not the solution in Paul's situation. He does have some authority, as when he performed an exorcism in Acts 16:16–18. But Paul's authority is not unlimited.

As far as we know, Paul died with his challenge, but the demon who is clearly his enemy, who wants to destroy him, who is thoroughly and irredeemably evil, becomes an asset to Paul. Why? God accomplishes His purposes in Paul's life because of the persecution and harassment. Paul goes well beyond enduring. He says, "I will boast all the more gladly of my weakness." This is not a stoic endurance. Paul realizes he asked for a kernel, but God gave him a harvest. He asked for a trinket, but God gave him true wealth. He sees his trial from God's perspective, and he delights that God said no to his original request.

Let us suppose someone asks you to carry a hundred pounds. Some of us cannot carry half that much. Quite frankly, I would prefer not to even try. But let's suppose you also agree that you cannot do it. You are then faced with two ways to remedy the situation. A very strong friend (God) comes along and says, "I will remove some of that weight. It is no longer a hundred pounds or even fifty. It's now twenty." You find twenty pounds to be much more doable.

But a burden is made bearable in another way too. Yes, God can lighten the load, but other times, God says, "I am going to ask you to carry the load, but I am also going to give you the shoulders upon which you can carry it. I am going to strengthen you." Sometimes God lightens the load; other times, He gives us strength to carry it. He will either lighten the load, or He will supply the grace for you to bear it.

Life-Changing Lessons for Praying People

What are the truths from this text that impact our lives today? Why should we be changed forever because we have read this chapter? I think God wants to change us today so we never look at our thorns in quite the same way again.

Here are three life-changing lessons.

With Burdens Come Blessings

Yes, God does not willy-nilly give you a burden without giving you grace and a blessing. We often wonder why a thorn will not be taken away. Friends, God has a reason for our thorns: growth in God's grace, strength, and power. He works the most in our weakness. It really does not matter how heavy our burden is if someone else carries it for us. Out of our weaknesses, we often bless others.

In 1869, Hudson Taylor, the great missionary to China, wrote to his sister Amelia:

> *The sweetest part . . . is the rest which full identification with Christ brings. I am no longer anxious about anything, as I realize this; for He, I know, is able to carry out His will, and His will is mine. It makes no matter where He places me, or how. That is rather for Him to consider than for me; for in the easiest position He must give me His grace, and in the most difficult His grace is sufficient. It little matters to my servant whether I send him to buy a few cash worth of things, or the most expensive articles. In either case he looks to me for the money and brings me his purchases. So, if God should place me in serious perplexity, must He not give me much guidance; in positions of great difficulty, much grace; in circumstances of great pressure and trial, much strength? No fear that His resources will prove unequal to the emergency! And His resources are mine, for He is mine, and is with me and dwells in me.*[2]

All this springs from the believer's oneness with Christ. "And since Christ has thus dwelt in my heart by faith, how happy I have been!"[3]

Even though his challenges were great, Taylor was at peace, trusting that God grants all His endless resources to him in Christ. And if we are servants of the Almighty, how can we be afraid with few (or many) burdens? Ultimately, we trust our Master to pay the bill, to supply every grace required for the task. Whether our burden is heavy or light, God will be there to meet our need. His grace will be sufficient.

I have frequently asked people to share when they have grown the most in their faith as a Christian. I have never had someone say, "It was during this peaceful time of my life when everything was going well. It was a season of prosperity, meaning, and joy. I have never grown in my walk with the Lord like I did during those days." No, no, no.

Instead, people will tell you about trials, difficulties, and seasons of hopelessness. Then God steps in. Sometimes, He lightens their load. Sometimes, He grants them strength. But God does His best work in our difficulties. And mature believers will admit, "I needed that trial, that burden. God changed my life through it. It was a blessing in disguise; my faith has never been the same since!" The first lesson is this: With burdens come blessings.

Burdens Are Specifically Chosen for Us

The apostle Paul shares, "A thorn was given *me* in the flesh." When it came, he was not initially thankful for it; he wanted a different gift from God. But God gave this thorn, specifically made for him.

As a preacher, I have worn plenty of suits. I have bought all of my suits off the rack in some department store. Nothing fancy. But more than forty years ago, I was in the beautiful city of Hong Kong, and a friend convinced me to have a suit tailor-made. So, I had one tailor-made suit that fit me perfectly for a while; but as the years went by, it began to shrink so terribly (putting on weight will do that to a suit!). Ultimately, my finest suit had to retire, so we gave it away.

Here's the point: When God sends a trial, it's not one just off the rack. It is tailor-made for you and me. Remember, you are number one on God's list of things to take care of in the universe, and so your trial is apportioned to you. "Paul, I gave *you* this thorn in the flesh. This one is yours; I have separate ones for others, but this one is yours." The tag says, "To Paul."

Do you realize that God is specifically interested in you? He is not only interested in the body of Christ as a whole but interested in each individual that makes up the body. God loves you. He wants you to walk with Him and know that your burdens are not random but specific for you.

Of course, we all need the help of others to carry our burden, to endure our thorn. We desperately need to "bear one another's burdens, and so fulfill the law of Christ" (Galatians 6:2). God has a purpose in your unanswered prayer.

Sufficient Grace Comes with Sufficient Faith

Let's be honest. Some of us are thinking, "God's grace is not sufficient for me." We are like a widow by the name of Doris. She loved her husband, but he died in his forties. She looked at other women in the church who were not madly in love with their husbands, and said to herself, "Why should I be widowed? These other women don't love their husbands as dearly as I loved mine." She parked her car in the church parking lot, dried her tears, came into church, sang the songs, did all the right things, got back into her car, and wept all the way home. And as she drove, she said to God, "Your grace is *not* sufficient. Your grace is *not* sufficient. Your grace is *not* sufficient!"

Are you going through a bitter divorce or a serious illness? I would wager that a lot of people reading this book are suffering pain. In church pews, in small groups, in Christian schools, and everywhere else, you can find Christians in pain. Some of them are saying, "God's grace is simply not sufficient." The reason I know some of you are thinking that is because there have been times when I have had such thoughts. There are times when it appears as if the promises just don't work. We often refuse to accept difficulty from God's loving hand.

What happened to Doris? During a time of spiritual revival in her church, she was invited into a prayer room with other women who would pray with her. She stayed an hour—a good length of time to get rid of the garbage, her bitterness, and her anger toward God. She dumped out, in her words, "cartfuls of self-pity" before the Lord. She came out of that prayer room and went on to give her testimony in churches around the country. What was her theme? "God's grace is sufficient."

One man to whom I told the story of Doris said he went through a similar time when he didn't believe God was there for him. "God let me have my temper tantrum," he said, "and then God used my failure, my trial and betrayal to lead me into a new season. And yes, I discovered that His grace was sufficient."

God's grace is sufficient, but you and I habitually fret with God. We worry. A woman flying for the first time was frightened to death. She constantly looked out the window at the jet engines, working herself into a frenzy of worry and fear. Finally, the young man next to her said, "Ma'am, if you want to sleep, I will watch over the engines for you." We often obsess, praying the same prayers over and over again, and then we investigate to see whether or not God is doing anything. It goes on and on. We will not commit and accept God's response. By how we act, we are expressing, "For me, God's grace is not sufficient." (See the appendix, "Prayers for 'Stuck' People," for more assistance if you feel stuck in this mindset.)

My wife, Rebecca, and I have often flown from Chicago to Frankfurt. Once you're on the runway or up in the sky, you can shout for someone to land the plane. You can press all the buttons, but it doesn't make any difference. Short of committing a crime, nobody is turning around and letting you off the plane. You are committed.

Let's suppose we're on a flight across the ocean. (You'll have to use your imagination because what I am going to describe is impossible due to security reasons.) I say to a flight attendant, "I think that the pilots might fall asleep. Would you go and check on them?" Then, because the attendant is kind, she entertains my concerns and checks on them. She returns a few minutes later and says, "Good news. You can relax because all three of them are awake."

"Great."

An hour passes and I start thinking, *People can fall asleep quickly. If one of the three fell asleep, the others might do the same.* So, I again ask the same flight attendant to check on them. I do it a third time, and she checks again because of her kindness. All is well.

An hour or two later, I strike up a conversation with her again, asking when the flight arrives, etc., then I say "Well, now that we're talking, would you check to see if the pilots are awake?" She is exasperated and says, "Let me make a deal with you. I will pour you a cup of coffee if you promise to step outside and drink it." Then she adds, "You are insulting the pilots of this plane!" And of course, I would be.

Brothers and sisters, you and I insult God, day after day after day. We commit something to God, and then we anxiously wonder whether God can be trusted. The anxiety increases as we fail to see God working as quickly (or as overtly) as we want. We continue to pray, pray, pray, and our prayers are nothing but an expression of our unbelief. Why? In our frenzy, we refuse to let the matter remain with God; we take it all back on our shoulders. We refuse to accept that God is in control, and we are not.

God's message to us today is this: "Wait on Me. I am at work. I will work it out, but it has to be on My timetable. Stop coming to Me with your timetable, your insistence that I do as you think I should." He continues, "I am already giving you grace. My strength and my power are prevailing in your weakness. But you must choose to accept it."

Paul accepted his situation; he made peace with his thorn. This thorn was subject to God's will. Paul accepted the situation and gladly thanked God for it: "Therefore I will boast all the more gladly of my weaknesses" (2 Corinthians 12:9). Paul refused to insult God by telling Him that He wasn't doing anything. Paul left the matter with God.

God is our pilot; we are on His plane, journeying with Him. He neither slumbers nor sleeps. Let us spend more time thanking and giving Him praise than we do constantly asking Him to do what we think He should. Yes, we intercede; we weep and we plead, but we also leave the final results to Him. There may be loss, regret, loneliness, and pain, but He will be with us through it. His grace will stretch like a rubber band and encompass our need.

"Commit your way to the LORD; trust in him, and he will act" (Psalm 37:5).

A Prayer to Accept Suffering

God is in charge of your sufferings. What is your greatest desire—the cessation of your difficulties or the increase of your spiritual growth? Do you want a life of ease or a spiritual revival? Would you willingly accept more suffering from the Lord if it meant a closer walk with Him? If not, you are likely too unpliable for revival. Yet if you trust in His Son, He is your Father, and He will eventually make you pliable, one way or another.

The book of Daniel mentions three friends: Shadrach, Meshach, and Abednego. In Daniel 3, King Nebuchadnezzar of Babylon says to them, "Bow down before this image. If you do not bow down before this image, I will throw you into the fiery furnace." We might find such demands to be strange, but persecution is never far away from God's people, even today. The three men give one of the most glorious, faith-filled responses in all of Scripture:

> "O Nebuchadnezzar, we have no need to answer you in this matter. If this be so, our God whom we serve is able to deliver us from the burning fiery furnace, and he will deliver us out of your hand, O king. But if not, be it known to you, O king, that we will not serve your gods or worship the golden image that you have set up." (Daniel 3:16–18)

They tell the king that the demand is not even worth discussing. The men are completely surrendered to the King of the universe, not Nebuchadnezzar. They accept anything that may happen to them. They believe that God can deliver them if He wants to. But if God doesn't rescue them, they are content to be people who die in faith, believing that God knows best.

The doctrine we must reclaim is providence. It teaches us that God's purposes prevail in and through the circumstances and hardships of life. For you to pick up this book on unanswered prayer, I suspect God probably has already directed various circumstances in your life that led to your pursuit of answers. Friend, God is using your trials. God's providence is doing its work, but the inner turmoil remains.

What do you want more, worldly peace or more grace?

God of our troubles,

You rule over all infirmities, even inconveniences.

You, Yahweh, make one mute, deaf, seeing, or blind (Exodus 4:11).

You form light and darkness, well-being and calamity (Isaiah 45:7).

You wrest peace from me.

On one hand, You wreck the hopes of the arrogant;

On the other, You weary the souls of the righteous.

Your sovereignty is inconceivable.

I cannot grasp it.

I dare not question it.

In such trials of suffering, dispensed from above, I ask and wait:

What is Your purpose? What is this suffering's end?

When will the discipline be completely wrought? Where is the grace You give?

You will supply an answer; You will teach Your will.

I accept Your work. Strike my flesh, refine my heart, upend my life.

Like Paul, I will choose to gladly receive Your grace (2 Corinthians 12:9).

Like Jesus, Your Son, I will learn obedience in this suffering (Hebrews 5:7–8).

In Jesus' name, Amen.

God in the Garden

Jesus and the agony of unanswered prayer

Two famous gardens appear in the Bible. There is the garden of Eden where the first Adam in a perfect environment said no to the Father. The second garden, the garden of Gethsemane, is where the second Adam, surrounded by hostility and excruciating agony, said yes to the Father.

On the brink of His betrayal and death, Jesus retreated to an olive grove called Gethsemane, which means "olive press." Within sight of the temple, Gethsemane sits just east of Jerusalem proper on the gentle slope of the Mount of Olives. Today, a small grove of olive trees still grows in that area. Around 10 or 11 p.m., Gethsemane is an ideal place to withdraw for prayer. For Jesus, this olive grove became an olive press as He was trodden and squeezed as a flower, its beautiful aroma rising to God. We almost want to take the shoes off our feet as we contemplate this passage of Scripture and realize we are eavesdropping on an agonizing prayer, the answer to which would determine our salvation.

Sometimes we think that Jesus is not really an example for us because He is God and we are not. Yes, He had a divine nature, but He also had a human nature; He was the God-man, but He didn't take refuge in His divine nature when He struggled physically and emotionally. We must see Him as a man struggling in Gethsemane; a unique man to be sure, but a man nonetheless.

You have probably read this many times before, but reread it as if for the first time.

> *And they went to a place called Gethsemane. And he said to his disciples, "Sit here while I pray." And he took with him Peter and James and John, and began to be greatly distressed and troubled. And he said to them, "My soul is very sorrowful, even to death. Remain here and watch." And going a little farther, he fell on the ground and prayed that, if it were possible, the hour might pass from him. And he said, "Abba, Father, all things are possible for you. Remove this cup from me. Yet not what I will, but what you will." And he came and found them sleeping, and he said to Peter, "Simon, are you asleep? Could you not watch one hour? Watch and pray that you may not enter into temptation. The spirit indeed is willing, but the flesh is weak." And again he went away and prayed, saying the same words. And again he came and found them sleeping, for their eyes were very heavy, and they did not know what to answer him. And he came the third time and said to them, "Are you still sleeping and taking your rest? It is enough; the hour has come. The Son of Man is betrayed into the hands of sinners. Rise, let us be going; see, my betrayer is at hand."* (Mark 14:32–42)

Do you feel Jesus' sorrow? His indescribable anguish? Mark, the author of this gospel, uses several words to convey Jesus' travail: distressed, troubled, and sorrowful, even to death. What an unusual Savior. He is not a Stoic or an emotionless hero. Jesus feels deeply, as any true human does. Who has not felt some sense of dread concerning a future event? And here is Jesus, preparing to endure psychological, physical, and emotional distress; in short, the weight of the sin of the world would shortly be upon Him. Understandably, He asks three of His disciples to come and be with Him, namely, Peter, James, and John, the same ones who had been with Him on the Mount of Transfiguration.

There are times when we want friends around us, especially when everything is so dark and so bleak and so hopeless we can't make it on our own. We are struck by Jesus' honesty; "My soul is very sorrowful, even to death." These are very strong words. He has a sorrow that is a killing kind of sorrow.

C. S. Lewis said, "Only He who really lived a human life (and I presume that only one did) can fully taste the horror of death."[1]

Thankfully, what Jesus faced is something we shall never have to face; even if we should die by crucifixion (highly unlikely of course), even if we were tortured to death, we can take heart that Jesus had a burden and agony unlike any other human being. He had a "cup" to drink.

In Matthew's account we read (and don't hurry over this): "And going a little farther he fell on his face and prayed, saying, 'My Father, if it be possible, let this cup pass from me; nevertheless, not as I will, but as you will'" (Matthew 26:39). We will never have to drink the cup Jesus did.

Four Questions That Beg for Answers

Jesus entered Gethsemane with an unimaginable weight, infinitely greater than any of us could bear. His betrayal, suffering, and crucifixion were only hours away, wherein He would redeem sinners from sin, death, and hell. This mission, the greatest of all missions, demanded prayer, and while He prayed alone, His three friends fell asleep.

His posture in prayer is unusual and desperate: "He fell on his face." In the NIV, it renders Matthew 26:39 as "he fell with his face to the ground." One does not always fall flat on their face in prayer, but we do see it elsewhere, for example, when the disciples understandably take this posture at the transfiguration. Here Jesus is overwhelmed with sorrow, uttering "loud cries" and desperately seeking His Father (see Hebrews 5:7). Jesus prays with His face in the dirt.

Perhaps Jesus is recalling Psalm 42:11: "Why are you cast down, O my soul, and why are you in turmoil within me? Hope in God; for I shall again praise him, my salvation and my God." Christ is in turmoil, but He depends upon His Father.

Amid sorrow, He trusts.

What Was the Cup Jesus Was Asked to Drink?

Let us listen in: "Abba, Father, all things are possible for you. Remove this cup from me. Yet not what I will, but what you will" (Mark 14:36). Considering that the disciples had time to fall asleep, this verse is a short summary of what was likely a long and difficult time of prayer. Mark's brief telling of Jesus' prayer begins with the Son saying "Abba," signifying His close relationship with the Father.

Was the cup simply the suffering Jesus anticipated on the cross? Have we ever stopped to think about how awful it must be to be nailed on a cross? Imagine Him being laid on a crossbeam, nails hammered through His wrists and feet, then the crossbeam is lifted up, and with a thud, it falls into the hole prepared for it.

There are some people who say the "cup" was the cup of suffering the terrifying death of crucifixion. But, of course, we know that can't be the complete answer because the Romans crucified many criminals, and some, despite the impending horror, faced their end with resolve.

In essence, the cup was the wrath of God that we deserve for sin. The Bible often uses this imagery to refer to God's wrath. Isaiah 51:17 mentions the cup of His wrath and in Revelation we read, that those who worship the beast and receives his mark "will drink the wine of God's wrath, poured full strength into the cup of his anger, and he [the apostate] will be tormented with fire and sulfur" (Revelation 14:10). The cup of His anger!

What a cup to drink! Jesus asks if there might not be another way; however, He knew He had to go through with the plans He and His Father made in eternity past. He who was sinless recoiled from the horror of becoming legally guilty of every sin imaginable and suffer for those sins.

Try as we might, we cannot grasp the terror of perfect holiness coming in contact with unimaginable wickedness. He who was with sinners in life is now going to stand in their stead in His death. There was no sin *in* Him, but the sins of the world would soon be laid *on* him.

The Bible teaches that hell is forever; and forever is endless. Now take the length of such suffering and compress it into three hours of darkness when Jesus was on the cross with the Father turning away from His own Son. Think of that.

Jonathan Edwards, the great theologian, said that Jesus Christ looked into the furnace of God's wrath and the fury, and knew it was into it that He soon would be thrown. He anticipated a horror we cannot grasp.[2]

Who Gave Him the Cup?

Jesus clarifies the answer to this question after Gethsemane was over and Jesus and His disciples were accosted by a mob wanting to arrest Him. Remember, Peter tried to cut off the ear of the servant of the high priest. Actually, we can quite rightly assume that Peter was aiming for his head but missed and just cut off his ear. Jesus responded, "Put up thy sword into the sheath," and then He said, "The cup which *my Father* hath given me, shall I not drink it?" (John 18:11 KJV).

Jesus didn't say, "The cup which the Sanhedrin has given to me, shall I not drink it?" He didn't say, "The cup, which Pilate is giving to me, shall I not drink it?" Nor did He say, "The cup, which Judas, inspired by Satan, is giving to me to drink, shall I not drink it?" We might expect Him to say, "The cup, which the Roman soldiers or the Jewish leaders are giving to me, shall I not drink it?" But Jesus doesn't say any of those things.

This cup was handed to Jesus by His Father.

God used all the different people and groups I just mentioned to do the terrible deed of nailing Jesus to the cross, but Jesus looked beyond the instruments God used and saw it as coming from His Father. Let us hear those words again, "The cup which *my Father* hath given me, shall I not drink it?" (John 18:11 KJV).

Jesus acknowledges the Father's supremacy and power. The Son has come to do the Father's will, and if another path could be found, the Father could find it.

What Was His Request?

His agonizing request was direct: "Remove this cup!" It was prayed three times. Jesus is asking, "Might there be some other way?" Of the many theological questions asked throughout the ages, a common one is whether the sacrifice of Jesus Christ was absolutely necessary. The question was whether God could have used some other blood, the blood of another person or even the blood of an animal to expiate sin. Well, the answer to that question is no.

In comparative religion classes in our universities, you will often hear statements like, "Christianity is no different from other religions. The gods of other religions also demand a blood sacrifice, such as the blood of an animal." True enough.

But—and this is critical—only in Christianity does God *become* the sacrifice! "God was in Christ, reconciling the world unto himself" (2 Corinthians 5:19 KJV). *God demanded blood, and because He is a Trinity, He was able to supply the very blood He demanded!*

It was either the shed blood of Christ or an aborted plan of redemption. There were no other options.

What Was the Response?

The request was not granted. "My Father, *if it be possible,* let this cup pass from me; *nevertheless,* not as I will, but as you will" (Matthew 26:39).

"Nevertheless, not as I will, but as you will."

Jesus does what no one wants to do—He submits. Everyone wants their own way, but Jesus does not. He voluntarily yields Himself to the will of the Father. This is a perfect example of Jesus "practicing what He preaches." He taught us to pray, "Your will be done"; and now in the most difficult of moments, at a time when one might suggest an exception, Jesus follows through. He says, "Not what I will, but what you will!"

There is no other way by which redemption could have been accomplished except that the holy Son of God came and shed His blood and died in our place. So, to return to the question, "Why believe in Jesus? Why not somebody else?" It was Jesus Christ's sacrifice alone, the sacrifice of the sinless man who was both God and man, that a holy God could accept. We have been redeemed "by the precious blood of Christ."

Jesus does what no one wants to do—He submits. Everyone wants their own way, but Jesus does not. He voluntarily yields Himself to the will of the Father.

Jesus prayed the same prayer three times. But the final answer was no. He would drink the cup of iniquity; He would accept the wrath we deserved; He would, for a time, be separated from fellowship with His Father, and cry out, "My God, my God, why have you forsaken me?" (Mark 15:34). The matter was settled—and settled forever. Jesus offered Himself and said He'd go through it. And thankfully He did because, if not, you and I would not be redeemed today.

In preparation for the horrible pain he was about to suffer Jesus would be offered a cup of compassion. We read that they mingled myrrh with some wine and gave it to Him (see Mark 15:22, 23). Apparently, this was to act as a sedative to dull His pain. But He rejected it, because He wanted to drink this cup of iniquity in all of its darkness and horror. *He drank every drop to the dregs.*

O Christ, what burdens bow'd Thy Head!
Our load was laid on Thee;
Thou stoodest in the sinner's stead,
Didst bear all ill for me.

Death and the curse were in our cup,
O Christ, 'twas full for Thee!
But Thou hast drained the last dark drop—
'Tis empty now for me.[3]

The planned redemption would move forward. The cup would be drunk in all of its fury and pain. The horror of the cross but also the triumph of the resurrection lay ahead.

Transforming Our Prayer Life

Brothers and sisters, contemplate His sorrow. In your struggle with unanswered prayer, do not turn away from the suffering Jesus. Turn to Him. He is *like* us. Jesus groans *with* us. He understands our sorrows. When He was about to go to the cross, He was travailing *for* us.

The lessons we learn are transforming.

Today's Prayerless Christians, Tomorrow's Backsliders

Where were Jesus' friends when He invited them to help Him bear His sorrow? His disciples were sleeping through their Master's agonizing cries for emotional and spiritual support. Yes, in a few hours, Jesus would be abandoned by His Father; but here in Gethsemane, He is abandoned by His friends. On the Mount of Transfiguration, Jesus in His dazzling beauty told Peter, James, and John about His "exodus" to take place in Jerusalem. They should have been on high alert, knowing how critical this hour was for their Master. Peter especially should have been beside Jesus in his hour of greatest need.

Just before Gethsemane, Peter affirmed:

> *"Even though they all fall away, I will not." And Jesus said to him, "Truly, I tell you, this very night, before the rooster crows twice, you will deny me three times." But he said emphatically, "If I must die with you, I will not deny you."* (Mark 14:29–31)

Talk about boldness and self-assurance!

So much for willpower. But even so, to stay up late on Passover was tradition. As one commentator says, "It was customary to stay awake late on Passover night and to speak of God's redemption . . . [the disciples] had probably stayed up late on nearly every other Passover of their lives."[4] But when Jesus needed them most, He found them sleeping! And Jesus is quite clear concerning His expectations. "Could you not watch one hour?" Was that too much to ask as His "hour" of suffering on the cross was approaching?

Jesus said, "Watch and pray that you may not enter into temptation. The spirit indeed is willing, but the flesh is weak" (Mark 14:38). In this context, "watch" means to be spiritually and physically alert. Why watch? We should watch to see if and when the enemy is coming. Parents should "watch" to see where Satan is gaining a foothold in the lives of their children; church leaders must "watch and be alert" over their congregations; and every one of us should "watch" over our own lives. If we are not alert, we will wander into Satan's territory without realizing it! Our enemy will provide all the comforts he can to distract us from devotion to Christ.

But with some churches canceling prayer meetings and many Christians giving only lip service to prayer is it any wonder that we are so intimidated that we fail to witness to our faith to those around us? Praise God that many of His people still pray; but in the US, the number of adults praying daily has recently slid from 58 percent to 46 percent (2012–2024).[5] Yes, indeed, the flesh is weak.

Today's sleepy and prayerless Christians are tomorrow's self-serving ineffective witnesses. Peter, James, and John were Jesus' closest friends. They saw the miracles, heard every sermon, witnessed the Father speaking to the Son, and much, much more.

But they weren't prepared for difficulty, and their lack of prayer showed it. By Mark 14:50, all the disciples flee. A few verses later, Peter denies Jesus.

A lack of prayer is a crisis. I understand that you are reading a book on unanswered prayer. Perhaps you're struggling with the temptation to simply give up and stop praying. Beware of where that path leads. I plead with you: Alertly and prayerfully remain with Jesus! Even if you doubt God and fight with disappointment, do whatever you must to cultivate spiritual watchfulness.

People occasionally come to me, asking how they could have a better quiet time. Their times of prayer are stale and lifeless. What advice do I give? The answer is not necessarily a popular devotional book from Amazon. In many cases, the problem is simple. People go to bed too late, often after watching shows or scrolling through social media on their smartphone or tablet. And when they wake up in the morning, they're still sleepy.

Judas was up and alert for the sake of silver coins. Are we up and alert for prayer, or can we not stay awake?

We cannot think we're better equipped than the disciples. Let us be alert in prayer! Let us go to sleep earlier, skip television shows, stop gaming for hours, recruit people who hold us accountable, and rearrange our whole day if it means we can pray. Judas was up and alert for the sake of silver coins. Are we up and alert for prayer, or can we not stay awake?

How should we be spending our morning moments in prayer? We should include worship, meditation, thanksgiving, interceding, and most certainly, submitting. In Gethsemane, the enemy of prayer was sleep! And that is still one of the great enemies of prayer.

Take stock of your prayer time this week. How much have you prayed? I shudder, for by evidence of our prayers (or lack thereof), too many people are only one more temptation away from denying Jesus. Take warning lest you shipwreck your faith and abandon the only Savior of souls! Prepare for times of testing by praying now. To repeat: Today's sleepy and prayerless Christians are tomorrow's backsliders.

From the Hands of God, Not the Hands of Men

Our cup (because we all have a cup God has asked us to drink) must be accepted from the hands of God, not the hands of man. Now I hope that you understand how the Scripture functions at this point and how theology works.

Jesus was delivered over to the hands of wicked men, but He was never out of the hands of God. There is only so much that wicked men could do. Wicked hands crucified Christ, but His last words on the cross were, "Father, into your hands I commit my spirit!" (Luke 23:46). The hands of the Father overruled the hands of wicked men.

Is there somebody in your life who wants to crucify you? Is there somebody who's out to get you, somebody who wants to minimize you, somebody who wants to put you in your place once and for all? You're angry with them, you're angry with your situation, and you say to yourself, "It's their fault." That may be true, but can you change your perspective and say, "The cup which *my Father* hath given me, shall I not drink it?"

You and I will look at our trials very differently if we take the cup of distress and unanswered prayer from the hands of God, not the hands of people or circumstances. I explained this to someone recently, and he said, "It is very difficult to get there, but once I arrived at that perspective, I was at peace."

Yes!

Joseph, who was sold into Egypt, saw past the cruelty and betrayal of his brothers, his heartbreak, loneliness, and tears and saw God. Years later when he revealed himself to his brothers he explained, "God sent me before you to preserve for you a remnant on earth, and to keep alive for you many survivors. *So it was not you who sent me here, but God*" (Genesis 45:7, 8).

He didn't merely say God took a bad situation and turned it into good . . . he said that the evil was part of God's plan. Of course the brothers remained fully responsible for their evil, but such is the mystery of the interaction between the actions of men and the overarching plans of God. You *sold* me, but God *sent* me!

Even as I type these words, I find myself pausing, thinking, and contemplating how things change when the cup of suffering is received from God, and not from people or events over which we have no control. Today, you are where God wants you to be, and if you begin to accept your circumstances from His hand instead of from the person who wants to harm you or the sickness that seeks to debilitate you, it will give you a whole different perspective. Our cup has been approved for us by our Father. It has passed through His hands.

Our Redemption Is Founded on an Unanswered Prayer

How I thank God for unanswered prayer!

What if God the Father had chosen to exempt Jesus from drinking the cup? What if He had honored the request, "Remove this cup from me"? What if the Father had said, in effect, "From what I've seen of humanity, they are so sinful and rebellious it's not worth it"? There would have been no suffering Jesus, no Savior on the cross, no perfect Man bearing the wrath of God in our place—if none of that happened, we would all be damned!

Please note this: *God's purpose in an unanswered prayer can be much greater than that of an answered prayer.* In this case, a no was not a loss but a win. Thank God for unanswered prayer! The single most important event in all of history—the death of Jesus and the saving of sinners—is founded upon unanswered prayer!

The single most important event in all of history—the death of Jesus and the saving of sinners—is founded upon unanswered prayer!

Just so, for us hearing a no from God may not be a loss but a win. At the end of the day, it's not really about us but about God and His purposes. We were all born with a sense of self-aggrandizement. We are all narcissists at some level. Our goal in life should not be happiness but holiness and obedience to God. To paraphrase William Barclay, "The love of God wants what is best. The wisdom of God knows what is best. The power of God can accomplish it."[6]

So, let us ask ourselves, what are we hanging on to, saying, "This is mine. I close my hand, and I refuse to open it for God"? Who are we to tell God that He has no right to say no? Or to question His love and justice when He does say no? *Sometimes suffering is the answer to our prayers!*

There is a song we used to sing in Canada, which isn't widely known in the United States, but I love the words. Let it be a testimony of all of us.

My Jesus, as Thou wilt!
O may Thy will be mine!
Into Thy hand of love
I would my all resign.

Through sorrow or thro' joy,
Conduct me as Thine own;
And help me still to say,
"My Lord, Thy will be done."[7]

How has the heavenly Father said no to you—your family, your dreams, your ambitions, your housing situation? He continues to grant you grace in the rejection, and He sustains you in the waiting. You pray for relief, just like Jesus. You cry, "Remove this cup from me!" But the cup is still there to drink. But it is He who hands it to us. Let us receive it.

And when we receive it from Him, we can choose to forgive and let go of our bitterness. Let us never forget that God uses unanswered prayer to develop our faith, to strengthen our resolve and to show us His grace in the midst of our disappointment.

Unanswered Prayers Are Not Unheard Prayers

Now the question is: Did God answer Jesus Christ's prayers? Yes, I believe that even His prayer in Gethsemane was answered. It's interesting that in the book of Hebrews it says, "In the days of his flesh, Jesus offered up prayers and supplications, with loud cries and tears, to him who was able to save him from death, and he was *heard* because of his reverence" (Hebrews 5:7). The Greek word for "heard" means that God responded to Jesus' prayers in Gethsemane. He was heard, though His immediate request was not honored.

In fact, Jesus cried that He might be exempt from death, and although the immediate answer to His prayer was the cross, three days after dying on the cross, He was triumphantly raised from the dead. Let's not hurry past this; consider the phrase "loud cries and tears." The Father heard the cries and saw the tears. I remember doing a home visitation, and a woman answered the door, quickly wiping the tears from her cheeks. "Forgive me," she said, "I just was praying for my son who is not walking with the Lord." I'm not sure what happened to her son, but I do know this, God saw and took note of those tears!

In the book of Revelation, we have a glimpse of how our prayers are preserved and are viewed as precious to God. We read that "the twenty-four elders fell down before the Lamb, each holding a harp, and golden bowls full of incense, which are the prayers of the saints" (5:8). So, a whispered prayer on earth is kept and brought as a gift before the Lamb and laid at His feet. Prayerful requests answered or unanswered on earth are recorded in heaven.

Unanswered prayers are not *unheard* prayers. Unanswered prayers do not mean that God is not listening, hearing, and caring. As we have learned repeatedly in this book, God does not answer our prayers with a cold no, but with "Yes, I hear you, but I have a larger plan." And though we are deeply disappointed we should say, "Your will be done."

I've heard preachers say you should never end a prayer with the words, "according to Your will" because it indicates you have not prayed in faith. But that's wrong. There are some prayers to which we do not have to add those words (such as the prayers Paul prayed for the church), but there are plenty of other prayers where we must add those words.

Jesus Was Abandoned That We Might Be Accepted

In Gethsemane, Christ is abandoned by His closest followers. But Jesus has not abandoned them . . . or you. As the old hymn declares,

For me it was in the garden,
He prayed: "Not my will, but Thine."
He had no tears for his own griefs,
But sweat-drops of blood for mine.
He took my sins and my sorrows,
He made them his very own.
He bore the burden to Calv'ry,
And suffered, and died alone.[8]

According to the Father's will, Jesus suffered for you. Even today, exalted at the right hand of God the Father, Jesus prays for you. He died precisely because He has come near to you. He prayed, "Not what I will, but what You will," and so accomplished our redemption. In a world filled with disappointments, abandonment, loneliness, despair, and hopelessness, Christ came for us—and He will never abandon us. He is not far off. And we can claim this promise: "Let us draw near with a true heart in full assurance of faith, with our hearts sprinkled clean from an evil conscience and our bodies washed with pure water. Let us hold fast the confession of our hope without wavering, for he who promised is faithful" (Hebrews 10:22–23).

We need a wake-up call. Many of us claim to have followed Jesus for years, but we've grown sleepy. We are content with our lives, and our bellies are full. We are more likely to be found sleeping than praying in the morning hours. Why does God not answer our prayers? *Maybe unanswered prayer is an alarm clock jolting us awake.*

In the name of Jesus Christ, I summon your conscience: Do not turn this page until you are prayerfully awake and yielded afresh to your Lord.

When the Father says no, we can trust Him, for He is still good. "If possible—but if not, Your will be done!"

A Prayer for God's Will to Be Done

Father,

What are You doing?

Where are You leading?

Why do You tarry as I suffer?

I confess that I do not understand Your ways,

I do not see Your designs, blinded by my circumstances.

I hesitate to hope in the world to come, shortsighted as I am.

I fail, yet I trust in Jesus afresh.

I fail, but You have not failed me.

I want to give up, but You have not abandoned me.

My flesh is weak, and my spirit feels weak too.

But by Your Spirit at work within me, I say, "Your will be done."

In Jesus' name, Amen.

Managing the Disappointment of Unanswered Prayer

When faith is stretched to the breaking point

God hasn't done me any good!"

That's what a Christian man said angrily to me when he was trying to cope with the bitter disappointment of praying with expectancy for a child who nonetheless died. I read about a quadriplegic who said: "Knowing God had the power to heal me but wouldn't made me very bitter. I would read passages like Isaiah 53:5 and 1 Peter 2:24, accusing God of holding the promise of healing before me like a piece of meat before a starving dog. He tempted me with the possibility, but He never enabled me to reach it."

How do we continue to believe in a God who *could,* but *won't*?

Even as I am writing this, our news media is filled with an endless number of heartbreaking stories about a huge, unexpected flood in Texas that swept away a Christian camp along with much of the surrounding region, resulting in the drowning of well over a hundred people, many of whom were children.

Let's not hurry over this. By the time you are reading this book, this tragedy will have long since faded from the news cycle, but for hundreds of parents and relatives, this nightmare will never end. Imagine as a parent, sending your precious son or daughter to a Christian camp where they will have supervised fun, be taught the Scriptures, and learn to pray. And then the news comes: Your child has been swept away with an unexpected torrential flood, and your child's body is found days later miles down the river.

Adding to your grief are a dozen questions for which there will never be totally satisfying answers. Why did the weather service not send out alerts earlier? Why did the camp staff not evacuate the camp at the first hint of danger? Added to these questions will be others, more personal discussions as to why you sent your child to camp in the first place and so on. I can imagine that in some homes, there was a difference of opinion, perhaps the father didn't want to send their child to camp, but the mother insisted, so now the blame game will go on for years to come.

But as a Christian, the question that will haunt you even more is: *Where exactly was God when my child needed Him? After all, the weather is ultimately under His control.* Yes, Satan brought both lightning and a windstorm to kill Job's children, but it was done under the strict control of God. So, where was He? And what difference does it make if "even the hairs of your head are all numbered" (Matthew 10:30), but when push comes to shove, God is not there to rescue you in the moment of greatest need?

Be assured that questions like this have plagued Christians since the beginning of time. Does faith in God work or doesn't it? Do we have a right to expect reasonable protection from God the Father toward His children? We know parents who asked that question years after their daughter was tragically killed in a traffic accident, causing her siblings to lose their faith in God. I know parents who asked that question after their daughter was sexually assaulted while doing mission work in downtown Chicago. The crime ruined her future emotional and spiritual stability.

And then I received an email from a very articulate woman in her forties who wrote to me about her spiritual journey detailing the emptiness she had experienced throughout the years as she'd been pursuing God since she was a child. Just read a few snatches of it.

> *I do not struggle with the basic doctrines of the Christian faith, but I doubt God's personal love for me. I pray continually, but I do not feel His presence; I do not feel comforted, I do not feel the "peace that passes understanding." I am seeking but not finding. Shouldn't I have encountered God by now? I feel as if I am praying into a void. I know all the promises in the Bible, but none of them feel true for me. I constantly live with unmet desires and dreams. I have kept myself a virgin, desperately clinging for purity for my wedding day, but I have never married. I long for a husband so much that I feel the grief of it; I mourn motherhood every day. I feel unbearably lonely. Sickeningly so. Shouldn't my faith anchor me rather than confuse me?*

Disappointment festers in such experiences, when God does not appear to heal, to care, and to reveal His presence. Christians have often wondered where God was. After all, they are the sheep of His pasture—so where is the Shepherd?

Bitterness. Anger. Silent disgust.

Where is God? I don't know about you, but I have spent time in hospitals, visiting the sick and dying. When I witness a child suffer or watch a young mother die of cancer leaving children behind, it is difficult. In those times, our faith can easily erode, and we wonder whether we can go on believing in the existence of a trustworthy God.

What can we expect faith in God to do, or not do? Must we see miracles in order to believe God is faithful?

When Life Is Hard and Answers Are Few

Let's take the time to focus on the faith of a group of believers described in Hebrews 10, who suffered times of great testing without seeing any deliverance. In the midst of persecution, the heavens appeared silent, and they died an untimely death.

No doubt these believers cried to God for deliverance with the expectancy that their enemies would be put to flight and life could resume to normal. But it was not to be. Fathers were killed while mothers and children lived; sometimes both parents died and children were left orphans. Life everywhere is cruel and hard.

The book of Hebrews was written to encourage early Jewish Christians from returning to Judaism. Because of their conversion to Christianity, they were not only marginalized but persecuted. And God did not appear to deliver them.

Let's read the text:

> *But recall the former days when, after you were enlightened, you endured a hard struggle with sufferings, sometimes being publicly exposed to reproach and affliction, and sometimes being partners with those so treated. For you had compassion*

on those in prison, and you joyfully accepted the plundering of your property, since you knew that you yourselves had a better possession and an abiding one. Therefore do not throw away your confidence, which has a great reward. For you have need of endurance, so that when you have done the will of God you may receive what is promised. (Hebrews 10:32–36)

Their commitment to Jesus subjected them to public humiliation; we read they were "publicly exposed to reproach and affliction" (v. 33). When the Communists took over China, pastors were paraded down the streets, even holding Bibles that had been torn in two. They were humiliated, publicly exposed, and treated as people of reproach. In Albania, the Communists tied pastors and priests together and forced them to walk down the streets while insults and excrement were hurled at them.

Some of the believers described in the book of Hebrews could have avoided suffering but nevertheless identified with those who were targeted. They suffered voluntarily, "being partners with those so treated. For you had compassion on those in prison, and you joyfully accepted the plundering of your property" (vv. 33–34). Imagine! Some could have avoided persecution but because they identified with those who were being persecuted, both groups suffered. There is something very noble about *volunteering* to suffer.

I heard Chuck Colson (Nixon's political aide turned evangelical leader) suggest that when the Holocaust took place in Germany, it would have been fitting for the Christians to join the Jews in their suffering. Imagine if two or three Christians voluntarily joined the Jewish people in those freight cars and went to their death identifying with those who were being so severely mistreated. I suspect there wouldn't be a lot of volunteers for such an assignment. But back in the early centuries of Christianity, some Jewish Christians could have sidestepped the suffering of their time but instead were willing to take up the cause of others who were being put to death! Quite frankly, this puts many of us to shame.

Where was God then?

How did these believers in Hebrews 10 respond? The text says, "You *joyfully* accepted the plundering of your property" (v. 34). Many of us cannot comprehend the devastation when mobs came and destroyed their families and their homes. They *joyfully* accepted it!

Let's let that sink in.

I don't know of any American, myself included, who would joyfully accept the plundering of their house or property. However, understandably, these Christians were becoming discouraged, because the author writes, "Therefore do not throw away your confidence, which has a great reward. For you have need of endurance, so that when you have done the will of God you may receive what is promised" (vv. 35–36). The Scripture speaks into their trial: "You need endurance. You accepted the trial well. You have run well this far. But as the persecution drags on year after year, you will become weary."

No doubt, they cried to God, begging, "God, deliver us. Make this right!" But they died without a miracle. No wonder they were on the verge of "throwing away their confidence." I have met Christians who threw away their confidence in God's promises because they lived with injustice and unanswered prayer for so long.

We've all probably heard someone say something like, "If there is a God in heaven, clearly, He doesn't care. I am finished." Christians have even thrown away the faith they professed because of other Christians. They have told me, "I did some work for that other Christian and he never paid me." Or, "The church is so full of hypocrites, I can't stand it, they are so judgmental!" So, they deconstruct their faith, saying they don't want anything to do with Christians and therefore don't want anything to do with their God. I am doubtful, however, that Jesus will accept such an excuse for a wasted life.

This admonition in Hebrews 10 to "not throw away your confidence" is followed by the famous chapter of Hebrews that catalogs the heroes of faith. Let's turn there to find out what faith can do, but also what faith sometimes does *not* do.

Clearly faith in God often does not accomplish what we think it should. But let us never forget that these kinds of questions are intended to test our faith and give us an opportunity to press more closely into God to find comfort in our sorrow. The experiences of others in Scripture in similar circumstances will encourage and instruct us.

Three Facts About Faith

Peter, who tradition says was crucified upside down because he did not think himself worthy to be crucified like Christ, wrote these words, "The tested genuineness of your faith—more precious than gold that perishes though it is tested by fire—may be found to result in praise and glory and honor at the revelation of Jesus Christ" (1 Peter 1:7). So, let's look at this refining fire.

Faith Sometimes Changes Our Circumstances

Read through Hebrews 11 and you will be introduced to a list of heroes, many of whom experienced wonderful, undeniable miracles. Abraham and Sarah conceived a child when they were beyond the age of childbearing. As for Moses we read, "By faith the people crossed the Red Sea as on dry land, but the Egyptians, when they attempted to do the same, were drowned" (Hebrews 11:29). What a miracle! Moses stands with his staff in hand, and God parts the waters!

The author of Hebrews moves forward to the conquest of the promised land. "By faith the walls of Jericho fell down after they had been encircled for seven days" (v. 30). We could spend hours speaking about miracles from the Old Testament. The author knows it too, so he says in verse 32, "And what more shall I say?"

The text summarizes God's miraculous deeds.

> *And what more shall I say? For time would fail me to tell of Gideon, Barak, Samson, Jephthah, of David and Samuel and the prophets—who through faith conquered kingdoms, enforced justice, obtained promises, stopped the mouths of lions, quenched the power of fire, escaped the edge of the sword, were made strong out of weakness, became mighty in war, put foreign armies to flight. Women received back their dead by resurrection.* (Hebrews 11:32–35)

This passage mentions or alludes to dozens of miracles. Consider the different kinds of miracles. The women who received their dead back to life refers to the days of Elijah. That is an incredible miracle of healing! Miracles of protection also appear as God delivers His people. He "stopped the mouths of lions" reminds us of Daniel 6. The different kinds of miracles continue to pile up as we consider healed relationships and unusual successes in battle wherein God miraculously gave the victory.

But that's not the story of everyone who has faith. Some die tragically, inexplicably, with no heroic story to tell. Some were forcibly drowned, thrown from cliffs, or stoned to death. They have no answers, just a list of unanswered questions.

And now comes a break in the content of this remarkable chapter.

Faith Sometimes Does Not Change Our Circumstances

Go slowly here.

In the middle of verse 35, the writer changes directions, "*Some* were tortured . . . *others* suffered mocking and flogging, and even chains and imprisonment."

When the manuscripts of the New Testament were written, they didn't have chapter or verse divisions. Those were added later to make it easier to find various passages. In a few instances, the verse divisions are inconvenient.

In my opinion, there should be a verse break in the middle of verse 35 due to the change of subjects. The entire chapter turns a corner as now we encounter people of faith who experienced no miracles at all. Let's begin in the middle of verse 35,

> *Some were tortured, refusing to accept release, so that they might rise again to a better life. Others suffered mocking and flogging, and even chains and imprisonment. They were stoned, they were sawn in two, they were killed with the sword. They went about in skins of sheep and goats, destitute, afflicted, mistreated—of whom the world was not worthy—wandering about in deserts and mountains, and in dens and caves of the earth. (Hebrews 11:35–38)*

Where are the miracles of deliverance?

There are none. Nothing but horrible persecution, poverty, homelessness, and eventual death. "They were sawn in two," evidently a reference to Isaiah, the great prophet. At least Jewish tradition tells us that the wicked King Manasseh ordered the murder of the prophet in this grotesque fashion. Wasn't Isaiah a person of faith? Why didn't God come to his deliverance?

The author then mentions how some people wandered about in goatskins, lived in caves, endured poverty, and suffered persecution. The allusion is to the time of the Maccabees. The Greek Empire fractured after the death of Alexander the Great. The land of Israel was under the dominion of the Seleucids. One of their kings, by the name of Antiochus IV Epiphanes, came into the land of Israel and offered a sow on the altar to insult the Jews. He even erected a statue of the Greek god Zeus in the temple![1]

The Jewish Maccabees led the resistance against such foreign oppressors in the second century BC. A horrendous persecution of the Jewish people then followed. The details are gruesome, but you can read historical examples in 2 Maccabees 7—an edifying read though not a canonical one. But back to our question: Where was God when *that* was happening?

Faith sometimes changes our circumstances; other times it doesn't. Sometimes there are miracles, and sometimes there aren't. Across the world today, more Christians have been martyred in the last century than during the days of the early church. Thousands of people have been put to death; churches filled with worshipers have been torched. Children have been stolen from their parents, and famine has ravaged whole regions where both Christians and non-Christians reside. Those who trust in God suffer in this life just as much as those who believe in a different religion or no religion at all.

Have you heard of The Voice of the Martyrs? This organization publishes a magazine, and you can learn a lot on their website.[2] I highly recommend that Christians understand what is going on throughout the global church. Richard Wurmbrand (1909–2001), who has spoken at The Moody Church, started the ministry. He was imprisoned in Romania many years ago under Communism. And thanks to his leadership, the website and magazine detail the numerous persecutions around the world.

Let me share one story:

I've often read stories about Christians who have had to dig their own grave even as they pleaded for their release. Then, sometimes a noose is put around their neck, and they're strangled to death before being thrown into the grave. Recently, I was in a country where we were shown a torture chamber and a room connected to it. When it was in use hundreds of years ago, the screams of the Christian being tortured would be heard by the prisoner in the adjoining room, a brother in the faith, knowing he was next. Horrific.

Our brothers and sisters are crying up to God for deliverance and are not seeing the walls of Jericho fall. When famines come and floods ravage their farms, they aren't witnessing the Red Sea part. They cry, "God, where are you? Save our families. Deliver us." And for the most part, they see little deliverance, though God does occasionally intervene.

We love to tell the story of Daniel and when God closed the mouths of lions. It is a true story. But my wife and I have been to Rome, and we have walked through the Colosseum and the Circus Maximus where so many followers of Christ were thrown to animals, and no angel came out of heaven to close the mouths of those hungry beasts.

Faith sometimes changes our circumstances; sometimes it doesn't. So, what is the big lesson of Hebrews chapter 11? Keep reading.

Faith Does Not Judge God by Circumstances

The purpose of Hebrews 11 is not just to show what miracles faith has wrought, *it is to show that you can be a hero of faith without seeing a miracle.* The faith that is "more precious than gold" (1 Peter 1:7) doesn't abandon faith in God when prayers go unanswered. This second category of people are also heroes of faith, perhaps even more worthy than the ones who saw the miracles. As people of faith, they believed that God was doing right by them even though He didn't deliver them. They died in faith, not judging God by their circumstances. We are assured that "they were commended through their faith" (v. 39).

We can never fathom the mystery of God's ways. We die without seeing many of the promises fulfilled. In Acts 12, James was beheaded by Herod. We have good reason to believe that the church was praying for his release, but their prayers were unanswered. James, the son of Zebedee, was beheaded and joined Stephen in martyrdom.

But a few verses later, we read that the church prayed for Peter who was scheduled for execution the next day, but that night God delivered him by an angelic rescue. If we think the church prayed with great faith, we would be wrong. For when Peter showed up at the door where the prayer meeting was being held, Rhoda answered the door. When she announced Peter was there, the rest of the believers didn't believe her.

Both James and Peter were in prison. One was rescued and one was not. Surely, circumstances like these tempt us to judge God. So often we ask: Why did this person get to live and another die at a young age? We have no inside information as to how to interpret these events.

Blessed are those who keep believing when God's way in the world is mysterious and for us, frequently filled with inexplicable suffering. Let me suggest you get used to the idea that God is going to treat others differently than he treats you!

How to Keep Believing When Heaven Appears Silent

I want to highlight six important truths to keep us grounded so we will not "throw away our confidence" in order to help us manage our disappointment with unanswered prayer and to do so with growing confidence.

Let Your Disappointment with God Draw You to Him

Let me ask: If you abandon your faith, do you think your life would go more smoothly? Where would your hope lie? Rather than abandon God, cry up to Him for comfort. "Blessed be the God and Father of our Lord Jesus Christ, the Father of mercies and God of all comfort, who comforts us in all our affliction, so that we may be able to comfort those who are in any affliction, with the comfort with which we ourselves are comforted by God" (2 Corinthians 1:3–4). The God who allowed the tragedy is the same God who comforts us as we pass through it.

Jesus did not promise us a life free of suffering. He promised us otherwise: "I have said these things to you, that in me you may have peace. In the world you will have tribulation. But take heart; I have overcome the world" (John 16:33). That's a promise we don't quote often! "In the world you shall have tribulation."

Every promise of God is "yes and amen" (2 Corinthians 1:20) in Jesus Christ, but we need to realize that until we see Jesus face-to-face we live with unfulfilled promises. Nothing was wrong with the promise God gave to Abraham about inheriting the land with specified boundaries (Genesis 12:1–3). But Abraham ended up having to purchase a burial plot for Sarah in that land; he died not having seen the fulfillment of what was promised. Will Abraham receive what was promised? Yes, he will. But he died without seeing the answers to his hope and prayers.

Believe Suffering Is God's Will

Let us return to the suffering saints of Hebrews, "For you have need of endurance, so that when *you have done the will of God* you may receive what is promised" (Hebrews 10:36). God is saying, "I realize your homes are being plundered. Your property is being stolen. But for you, My will is for you to endure!"

We are called to follow Jesus, and we must endure on the path that God has mapped out for us. No escape hatch existed for Jesus in the garden of Gethsemane, and there are times when one doesn't exist for us. Sometimes that suffering is simply a part of our calling as believers, "For it has been granted to you for the sake of Christ you should not only believe in him but also suffer for his sake" (Philippians 1:29).

We must ask ourselves: Am I able to accept this heartache if I know it has come to me from my Father in heaven and not some random force of nature or the happenstance of uncontrolled events? Would you not agree that we can endure much more faithfully if we know that our pain and sorrow was given to us from Christ rather than simply the result of injustice that is out of control? I am comforted when I realize that the God who loves me is firmly in charge, and as is often said, He keeps His hand on the thermostat.

Of course there are different kinds of suffering. For some, God has physical affliction mapped out for them; for others, it is the suffering of financial loss, the pain of relationships gone sour, the burden of unrealized expectations, or the sorrow of a loved one's passing. Whether the suffering is the result of our own foolishness or circumstances beyond our control, we must ask God for wisdom to make the next move. We must pray, "God, even if I did not sign up for this give me grace to follow Your will in the days and years I have left."

We Must See Our Suffering in the Context of Eternity

We must have the deep conviction that the eternal invisible world is exponentially more important than this passing visible world. In the minds of many of us in Western cultures, eternity is often undervalued. In Romans 8:18, Paul says, "For I consider that the sufferings of this present time are not worth comparing with the glory that is to be revealed to us." In 2 Corinthians 4:17, he adds, "For this *light momentary* affliction is preparing for us an eternal weight of glory beyond all comparison." If you are suffering today, that truth can be difficult to accept; but Scripture calls your suffering "light" and your trials "momentary." In comparison with eternity, our suffering is *light*. But we must compare it with the eternal *weight* of glory.

In a sense, Paul is saying, "On one side of a scale, place all of your affliction and all the things God has not done for you. That side would weigh a mere feather. On the other side, the eternal weight of glory would be like an elephant stepping on the scale." That difference is the proper context for our life's suffering—the eternal weight of glory that awaits every Christian.

But these early Christians did it. God could have delivered them, yes. But instead of being bitter, they suffered joyfully and confidently. God had something better in mind for them, and so they endured the trial. Why? They truly believed in the nearness of the world to come. It was so real to them they could say, "All the things of earth have been weighed in light of the coming of our eternal fellowship in the presence of God."

As Christians, we must ask ourselves whether we are living for the present world, carefully guarding and hoarding what is passing away. Or are our lives focused on the life to come?

There is a story that's told about prisoners in a World War II concentration camp who were starving to death, barely surviving in horrendous conditions we can scarcely describe. Suddenly, joy broke out, and they began to sing and laugh. Word had leaked into the prison that World War II was over. Deliverance was on the way. They were still in prison, but they rejoiced as if they were free. Why? Their suffering was only for a short while longer.

If the suffering is nearly over and deliverance has almost arrived, you can endure and you can do so with joy. In essence, the Christians in our text said, "We have heard from another world. News has been leaked to us that Jesus is Lord. He is King. He is God. Someday soon, He is going to arrive, but for now, we can joyfully accept the plundering of our property because we know we have property in heaven beyond the reach of our enemies."

Why could the heroes of faith accept the bitter disappointment of unanswered prayer and their untimely death? Once again, we have to emphasize that they looked beyond this life to the next; eternity was infinitely longer than time, and they knew that the ultimate and greatest faith is to look beyond their circumstances to God.

When faced with a crisis, let us pray for grace to be able to pray something like this:

> *God, I know You are able to heal my family member. I recognize You are able to resolve this situation. But if You do not, let angels, demons, and all creation know that I will not swerve in my commitment to You. I am steadfast because faith is not merely receiving from You the things that I*

> *want. I place my faith in You and will receive whatever You give me. Let it be known that I will continue to believe.*

Back to Hebrews 10. What was the reward these Christians were to receive if they were faithful? Let's look at several ways in which the text describes the rewards:

"You knew that you . . . had a better possession" (v. 34).

Your confidence "has a great reward" (v. 35).

"You have need of endurance, so that when you have done the will of God you may receive what is promised" (v. 36).

"Yet a little while, and the coming one will come and will not delay" (v. 37). (This is a reference to the return of Jesus. We have to let a blessed eternal future give us hope and comfort in the painful present world.)

Live by Promises, Not Explanations

To the young woman who wrote to me saying she has no sense that God loves her, I would encourage her to remember that feelings, though important, sometimes lie to us. To her and to all of us—myself included—I would prayerfully ask her to read promises such as the following, reminding ourselves that Jesus may not have *felt* the Father's love for Him when He hung on the cross but no doubt still *believed* His Father loved Him.

> *Who shall separate us from the love of Christ? Shall tribulation, or distress, or persecution, or famine, or nakedness, or danger, or sword? As it is written, "For your sake we are being killed all the day long; we are regarded as sheep to be slaughtered."No, in all these things we are more than conquerors through him who loved us. For I am sure that neither death nor life, nor angels nor rulers, nor things present nor*

> *things to come, nor powers, nor height nor depth, nor anything else in all creation, will be able to separate us from the love of God in Christ Jesus our Lord. (Romans 8:35–39)*

Will being killed separate us? No, the sword cannot sever us from Christ. Will sickness separate us? Sickness cannot. Will angels separate us? Angels cannot. Will demons separate us from the love of Christ? Demons cannot. Will anything in all of creation separate us? No, it cannot. No matter the circumstances we face, no matter whether we live or die, we are beloved by Christ. Let us keep on believing, come what may.

Faith is not merely receiving from God what we want, it is also accepting whatever God gives us.

Faith is not merely receiving from God what we want, it is also accepting whatever God gives us. Please understand that such acceptance might take time and great emotional struggle. And of course, justice should be pursued when possible. But tragedy is often best accepted by realizing that God is working in ways we do not have to understand.

One angry and hurting woman said to her pastor, "Where was your God when my son was killed?" The pastor poignantly replied, "He was on His throne—the same place where He was when *His* Son was killed." In the previous chapter, we saw how Jesus accepted the will of God, no matter how piercing the torment. True faith is a deep and abiding trust in the Father.

To repeat: We can change some things (usually few), but many are beyond our control. However, nothing is beyond God's control. We commit ourselves to God and leave the decision with Him. The question that often follows is, "Does committing everything to God mean we shouldn't pray anymore?" No! We keep praying, but in faith. When we commit something to God, we pray even more about the matter, but our prayers are filled with thanksgiving, praise, and confidence. We pray without ceasing, but we keep taking the burden from our shoulders and putting it onto the One of whom it is said that "the government shall be upon his shoulder" (Isaiah 9:6).

In the process, we come in prayer preoccupied with our need, but we leave preoccupied with God. We believe that what God does *in* us is sometimes more important than what God does *for* us, as He teaches us to keep believing even without miracles.

Pour Out Your Sorrow and Disappointment to God

To those dear parents in Texas who lost children during that terrible flood, we know they will rightly grieve until the day they die. But as believers, they can grieve with hope. We have many promises still to be fulfilled after our death. *Sickness* here, but *health* over there; *injustice* here, but *perfect justice* in the world to come; *rejection* here, but a warm *welcome* over there; *unanswered questions* about the flood over here as we look "through a glass, darkly," but then "face to face" (1 Corinthians 13:12 KJV).

So, I pray that those parents will run to God for comfort; that they will trust the God who, by allowing this terrible, torrential rain causing a river to rise by twenty-nine feet in forty-five minutes, took their precious children. Of course, God could have prevented the rain; of course, the flood could have come during the day rather than at night when the children were sleeping. Of course, knowing what was to come, He could have motivated the original visionaries to build their camp farther away from the river . . . of course, of course. And yet, *the families will need the very God who took their children; they need Him more urgently now than ever because He is "the God of all comfort."*

We can accept unanswered prayer because we believe God's will is best. We also know that the trial of our faith is more precious than gold. If we live that way, we will be in God's catalog of the heroes of faith who went to our death without seeing all of the promises fulfilled.

Cyprian, the great church historian and theologian, said that Christianity would never have encompassed North Africa in the early centuries were it not for the plagues that swept across the Roman Empire from AD 249 through 261. He said the plagues were the greatest blessing to Christianity, and the reason is because the Christians died differently than the pagans. When Christians died, their relatives and friends had the hope of being reunited with them someday. Amid their sorrow there was also the joy of knowing their loved ones were with the Lord. That's why many people turned from paganism and accepted Christianity.

Doubts Are Welcomed, and Blessedness Is Increased

Remember that our doubts are welcome, and God's promise is increased blessedness with increased faith.

Jesus gave a special blessing to those who did not abandon their faith even when they couldn't square what God did with what they expected. Among them was John the Baptist.

He was the forerunner of Jesus, a cousin in the flesh. He was a great man. Then suddenly, he was thrown into prison for rebuking Herod's sinful lifestyle. Here was John's problem: He knew the Old Testament and read Isaiah 61:1, "The Spirit of the Lord GOD is upon me, because the LORD has anointed me to bring good news to the poor; he has sent me to bind up the brokenhearted, to proclaim liberty to the captives, and the opening of the prison to those who are bound."

We can imagine that John wondered, "If Jesus is the Anointed One who came to proclaim liberty to captives, what am I doing here?"

John sent word to Jesus and asked, "Are you the one who is to come, or shall we look for another?" (Mathew 11:3). John is the last man you'd expect to have doubts! But he must have turned this idea over in his mind: "If Jesus were the Messiah, then I would be delivered. Those are the kinds of things that messiahs do. They deliver people." Thus, John sent a message to Jesus that he was expecting something better, something more consistent with the mission of Jesus.

Jesus responded not by rebuking John, but by affirming him, "There is no man greater than John the Baptist" (see Matthew 11:11). Jesus replied to John, "'The blind receive their sight and the lame walk, lepers are cleansed and the deaf hear, and the dead are raised up, and the poor have good news preached to them. And blessed is the one who is not offended by me'" (11:5–6).

Could I give you a Lutzer paraphrase? Jesus was saying, "John, blessed is the person who is not upset with the way I run My business. Blessed is the person who refuses to say, 'If God doesn't help me now, I will cease trusting in Him.' Blessed is the person who refuses to say, 'Because God didn't resolve this situation and deliver this person, I am never going to bother Him with another request again.' Blessed is the person who does say, 'I am going to pray and seek God. I am going to ask Him to deliver and provide miracles, but at the end of the day, I am going to be satisfied with how God runs His business.'"

We don't know whether Jesus' reply satisfied all of John's doubts, but what we do know is that he was later beheaded thanks to Herod's sensual insanity. Read the story in Mathew 14:1–11 and know that John died with the blessing of Jesus. And today, we can read the words of Jesus about John: "Among those born of women there has arisen no one greater than John the Baptist" (Matthew 11:11).

As for your doubts, tell God honestly why you have reason to doubt; He already knows why, but He wants to hear it from you.

I have quoted only a few verses from Psalm 77 here, but follow Asaph's lead as he prayed during days of trouble.

I cry aloud to God, aloud to God, and he will hear me.
In the day of my trouble I seek the Lord;
In the night my hand is stretched out without wearying;
My soul refuses to be comforted.

When I remember God, I moan;
When I meditate, my spirit faints.
You hold my eyelids open;
I am so troubled that I cannot speak. (vv. 1–4)

Asaph continues:

Then my spirit made a diligent search. . .
"Has his steadfast love forever ceased?
Are his promises at an end for all time?
Has God forgotten to be gracious?
Has he in anger shut up his compassion?"
Then I said, "I will appeal to this,
To the years of the right hand of the Most High." (vv. 6–10)

After you read Psalm 77 in its entirety, you'll notice that by the end of the poem, Asaph's faith in God was restored.

The author of Hebrews had the assurance these Christians will endure. He ends by saying, "But we are not of those who shrink back and are destroyed, but of those who have faith and preserve their souls" (Hebrews 10:39).

If you are hurting today and are disillusioned with God, I understand. Here's the bottom line: Faith always leads to ultimate victory. At the coming of the Lord Jesus Christ, we shall receive our new bodies, we shall receive justice, and we will enjoy the pleasures of God. For now, however, we must endure, because we read of the one who shrinks back, "my soul has no pleasure in him" (Hebrews 10:38).

God reserves His pleasure for the faithful. Hearing Jesus say, "Well done, good and faithful servant" will make all the suffering worth it.

Could I put it this way? I've heard it said that today we have a single drop of water, but the Bible says the day is coming when we are going to have the whole ocean. Today, we have the flower, but the day is coming when we will receive the entire garden. Today, we sample the hors d'oeuvres, but the Bible says that the marriage supper of the Lamb awaits us.

The wait is worth it! Let us follow the path of our suffering Savior to glory, trusting in our good Father, whether He answers our prayers or not.

Hebrews 10:38 mentions the righteous one, specifically "*my* righteous one." I love that. That possessive pronoun means much! God is saying, "*My* righteous one shall live by faith." The author of Hebrews was quoting Habakkuk 2:4, which is the verse Paul reiterates in Romans 1:17.

The righteous shall live by faith!

When we cannot understand God's hand, let us trust His heart. Eternity awaits.

A Prayer for Days of Dying

In June 2021, Scott was serving as a missionary teacher when the Delta variant of COVID-19 swept through the country of Zambia. The health department statistics woefully underreported what he experienced. Local pastors testified that bodies were piled outside of morgues. He lived next to the country's largest cemetery, and for the entire month of June, he and his family listened to funerals, all day, every day. Death came to his neighborhood. Here is Scott's prayer for such days. Let us join him in prayer, for sometimes God gives us days of dying.

Our God,

The Savior, yet also the judge,

The merciful One (Exodus 34:6), yet also Yahweh who smites (Ezekiel 7:9),

The giver of peace (Ephesians 2:14), yet also the bringer of calamity (Isaiah 45:7),

Lord, the tendrils of death are entangled about us.

Coffins, sicknesses, griefs, and lifeless bodies grip our thoughts.

Death is our birthright in Adam, yet we never expect to inherit.

We are coddled and self-deluded by comfort and safety until You arrive with our body bag.

Wickedness resides within us.

Either we kill sin or sin kills us.

If our funeral delays, if our body does not
decay, may we die a better way—

Confessing our spiritual ills,

Mortifying our wrath-provoking wrongs.

God, while hospitals sweep out the
dead, may I weep out my sins.

In days of death, You set beauty
in the land of the living.

In Christ, hope, goodness, and holiness
burst forth from the grave.

I die with Him today; my inner flesh lies in state.

I rise with Him today; the Spirit vivifies my mind.

Raised with Christ, help us to kill our sin.

We long for a better death in days of dying.

May we die to sin and live by Your Spirit.

In Christ we pray, Amen.

Getting Beyond Requests to God Himself

Entering His presence with anticipation

Attend a prayer meeting and you'll soon discover that most requests are for physical healing. This is understandable since our health is so important to us, and diseases, heart attacks, cancers, and strokes devastate our lives. Disappointment with such unanswered prayers can embitter us and breed cynicism. In the process, we miss the primary purpose of prayer and choose the path of prayerlessness, turning to other pursuits.

Before we discuss the challenge of accepting unanswered prayer, let me emphasize: Let us never give up praying just because we do not have our request answered. There are numerous testimonies of people who kept praying for years even against all odds and would not accept no for an answer and then years later their request was answered. God wants us to prevail in prayer, sharing our burden and our heart. But sometimes we just have to accept the reality that our prayer will never be answered; we will not live to see the desire of our hearts fulfilled.

So, what do we say to those disillusioned with unanswered prayer?

Let's take a deep breath and look at the bigger picture. What if the purpose of prayer is not just to get our needs met but to realize that our greatest need is God Himself? What if we have to shift our paradigm from the mentality of *getting* to the mentality of *relationship*? What if *getting from* God takes second place to *getting to know* God?

God is, after all, a God of joy. So, what if He invited us into His presence simply to enjoy Him, whether He gives us what we ask for or not? Whenever I am asked to personalize a book I've written, I reference these words, "Therefore my heart is glad, and my whole being rejoices. . . . You make known to me the path of life; in your presence there is fullness of joy; at your right hand are pleasures forevermore" (Psalm 16:9, 11).

If pursing God is our goal, we will be able to accept the disappointment of unanswered prayer more easily.

If pursing God is our goal, we will be able to accept the disappointment of unanswered prayer more easily. God will be there to comfort us even without explanations. I, personally, have discovered this paradigm shift can transform our prayer life into a time we earnestly long for; it will be a meeting with the Almighty whom we have come to love and serve.

John Piper is well known for saying that "God is most glorified in us when we are most satisfied in Him."[1] Henry Blackaby, a noted Bible teacher, said, "Watch to see where God is working

. . . immediately join Him!"[2] The experience of Job taught us that we don't have to understand in order to worship and believe. If you have nothing left, is God worth it even if you have none of His blessings? Every time we value God, choosing Him no matter what, we have worshiped.

Moving from Physical Needs to Spiritual Needs

John Paton had a praying father. The nineteenth-century Scottish missionary to the New Hebrides Islands grew up in a home with a small room where his father would retreat to pray at various times throughout the day. John said,

> *We children got to understand by a sort of spiritual instinct (for the thing was too sacred to be talked about) that prayers were being poured out there for us, as of old by the High Priest within the veil in the Most Holy Place. We occasionally heard the pathetic echoes of a trembling voice pleading as if for life, and we learned to slip out and in past that door on tiptoe, not to disturb the holy colloquy.*[3]

Ah, what a wonderful image of household prayer! Prayer like that transforms lives and displays God's glory to the world. It reminds me of the prayers of Paul for his spiritual children, the first churches across the Gentile world. Scintillating gems of intercession crown his letters; his paternal prayers reflect the wisdom of God's purposes and overflow with Christian love.

While Paul rightfully instructs the Philippian church to offer their requests to God (Philippians 4:6), Paul's prayers prioritize the spiritual growth and strength of His people instead of their physical well-being. It is curious that the first letter to Timothy mentions that Paul's spiritual son had "frequent ailments," but to our knowledge, Paul doesn't record a prayer for his healing (1 Timothy 5:23). While one could look at Paul's many prayers (including Philippians 1:9–11; Colossians 1:9–12; and 1 Thessalonians 5:23), his letter to Ephesus exemplifies his "inner being" priority in prayer. As you read this, just bask in the richness of what he prayed about. Paul says,

> *For this reason I bow my knees before the Father, from whom every family in heaven and on earth is named, that according to the riches of his glory he may grant you to be strengthened with power through his Spirit in your inner being, so that Christ may dwell in your hearts through faith—that you, being rooted and grounded in love, may have strength to comprehend with all the saints what is the breadth and length and height and depth, and to know the love of Christ that surpasses knowledge, that you may be filled with all the fullness of God. Now to him who is able to do far more abundantly than all that we ask or think, according to the power at work within us, to him be glory in the church and in Christ Jesus throughout all generations, forever and ever. Amen. (Ephesians 3:14–21)*

Much like John Paton's father, Paul is on his knees pouring out prayers for his Ephesian children. In contrast to a world that prioritizes the gratification and health of the outer being, Paul prays concerning their inner being, that they may have the power of the Spirit, a heart filled with Christ, and a mind that comprehends the boundless love of God. The Ephesian believers need to be "filled with all the fullness of God." They must become godly in the truest sense! Especially in a context filled with temptations to their old life of vice (see Ephesians 4:17–32), the apostle to the

Gentiles yearns that Christian virtues of love and faith root deeply in the Ephesians, springing forth into a Christian life, bringing glory to God through the church.

Friends, God hears our requests, and we rejoice when He chooses to heal our physical ills. Eschewing destructive habits and cultivating a life of wisdom, we should seek to maintain our outer being as a holy temple unto the Lord. Yet, let us not fail to recognize that the greatest challenges in our churches, our families, and our own selves begin in our *inner* being. And when we have a strengthened inner being overflowing with love and transformed by faith, the world beholds God's glory through us.

We need *inner* strength more than we do *outer* strength.

Seeking God

In a previous chapter, we highlighted the heroes of faith in Hebrews 11, showing that some of them saw miracles while others did not, yet both were commended for their faith. But we return to this marvelous chapter where we find one of the most important statements in all of Scripture. If this will not reprioritize our prayer life, possibly nothing will. Hebrews 11:6 says, "And without faith it is impossible to please him, for whoever would draw near to God must believe that he exists and that he rewards those who seek him." Greek scholars tell us that the emphasis means to "*diligently* seek Him." Some translations use the phrase, "diligently seek Him out."

And perhaps, for some reading this, the journey of pursuing God is going to begin today. So, let's try to answer the question, "What does it mean to have the faith to seek God out?"

The Object of Faith Is God the Creator

All faith needs an object; everyone has faith in someone or something. Many people claim they are not people of faith. They say, "I don't like this idea of faith. I accept only reason and science." That's nonsense. Everyone operates in faith. For example, you go to a doctor whose name you don't remember. He gives you a prescription you can't read. You take it to a pharmacist whom you've never met. He gives you a substance you've not analyzed and verified, and yet you take it. That is faith!

What God are we to seek? There are plenty of "gods" in our culture. But Christians are trusting in the God (with a capital G!) who created the universe (Genesis 1:1). We are invited to do on earth what we will do eternally in heaven, "Worthy are you, our Lord and God, to receive glory and honor and power, for you created all things, and by your will they existed and were created" (Revelation 4:11).

Yes, we come to fulfill the prayer of Jesus who prayed for us, "And this is eternal life, that they know you, the only true God, and Jesus Christ whom you have sent" (John 17:3). May it never be said of Christians that we have a small god. We have the one and only great God. He is the God who redeems. And this God is the one we seek.

And we seek Him because He first sought us!

Perhaps you have heard a fellow Christian testify, "I came to know Christ" or "I found Christ as my Savior." We understand what they mean, but strictly speaking, none of us found Christ. Christ found us! Not a single sheep on the planet goes looking for a shepherd. The shepherd looks for his sheep. The Good Shepherd found us. He is the God who redeems. He is the God who created, yes, but He's also the God who seeks, the God who finds, and the God who keeps.

In James 4:8 we read, "Draw near to God, and he will draw near to you." And Jesus, who came to earth to reveal the Father, said, "Come to me, all who labor and are heavy laden, and I will give you rest. Take my yoke upon you, and learn from me, for I am gentle and lowly in heart, and you will find rest for your souls. For my yoke is easy, and my burden is light" (Matthew 11:28–30).

And so we come willing to learn, willing to submit, and willing to worship. But we come also because of His Spirit working in us through His Word.

The God Who Rewards

"God rewards those who diligently seek him." God rewards! A form of Christianity exists that does not have a reward—a belief in a God who is reluctant to give or who must be appeased by our good deeds. He is the God of obligation, the God who is difficult to please. Some believe God exists primarily to condemn, to judge, and to interfere with our happiness. Why should we go to church? It is what we *ought* to do. Why should we read the Bible? It is what we *ought* to do. Why should we preach the gospel to the lost? It is what we *ought* to do.

Of course, we ought to do these things, but not out of a sense of obligation or thinking God is unhappy so we should try to appease Him. That kind of "ought to" Christianity is legalistic, and it is dead. Young people frequently leave the church and Christianity because they've only been introduced to an "ought to" kind of Christianity.

God doesn't pay us, but He does reward us.

Payment is a return dependent on how much you do, how much you earn. So, the question becomes: How long have you served God? How much money do you give? How many good deeds have you done? Like the elder brother in the story of the prodigal son, we expect to be paid for our efforts and are angry when we think we are short-changed.

In contrast, reward is based on grace; it is not earned, but rather a gift given out of proportion of what one would expect. The reward is God Himself. Have you ever awakened in the morning and discovered your heart is not "hot for God"? You have very little desire to seek Him; your mind is filled with pressing duties and circumstances that are beyond your control. So, what do you do?

At such moments of spiritual dryness, we look to the God of all grace. Tell Him the truth: "Lord, my heart is cold. I'm distracted because of all these matters of life. Therefore, Father, bring me into the joy and the gladness of this moment of worship and obedience." You diligently seek Him not based on your performance but upon grace. That is how we "seek Him out."

Earlier, we expounded on the faithful Christians in Hebrews chapter 10. Do you remember why people willingly gave up their homes and endured the plundering of their property? The text explained that they "had a better possession and an abiding one. Therefore do not throw away your confidence, which has a great reward" (Hebrews 10:34–35). Why did Moses leave the treasures of Egypt? He was looking forward to the reward!

That reward is the enjoyment of God in this life and personal fellowship in the very presence of God in the life to come. Yes, "in your presence there is fullness of joy " (Psalm 16:11). If you are burdened by disappointment with unanswered prayer, dive a little deeper into the joy that awaits you. We are told to "delight yourself in the LORD, and he will give you the desires of your heart" (Psalm 37:4).

Imagine a Christian life in which you experience a complete sense of accomplishment and fulfillment, not because of what you do but because of what Christ has done; you focus on His work, not your own. You walk with Him and love Him, enjoying the fullest sense of contentment and rest. Imagine!

David Brainerd (1718–1747) was a missionary among the Native American Indians in New England. During his brief life of ministry that has inspired numerous missionaries after him, he wrote in his diary describing one day when, "I enjoyed much of the light of God's countenance . . . and my soul rested in God."[4] He truly loved the presence of God. He also wrote, "One hour with God infinitely exceeds all the pleasures and delights of this lower world."[5] Let me share one more quote from his journal: "I desired nothing but himself; nothing but holiness that he had given me these desires, and he only could give me the thing desired."[6]

I can't read a quote like that without being convicted and rebuked in my heart.

God gives us a desire for Himself, and He is the only one who can fulfill the desires He gives. Scripturally, when you are born again, that transformation goes down to the level of desire. The people you love—spouse, family, close friends—are people with whom you are closely acquainted. You have spent time with them. Yet, speaking to Christians about Jesus, Peter says, "Though you have not seen him, you love him" (1 Peter 1:8). That love is birthed in our hearts by God.

A love for God, birthed in us by the Spirit of God, can displace our basest desires.

A man struggling with pornography wrote a long article talking about his on-again, off-again addiction. How was he finally able to break free? It was when he developed a desire to please God that was greater than his desire for this sin. As an example, he referenced the Sermon on the Mount; "Blessed are the pure in heart, for they shall see God" (Matthew 5:8). When Potiphar's wife tried to seduce Joseph, he resisted the temptation by having a right view of sin and a right view of God. "How then can I do this great wickedness and sin against God?" (Genesis 39:9).

Guilt and shame cut us off from fellowship with the God we love. Growing in our love for God is the best deterrent against sin. When we fail, we dare not let our shame drive us away from God, but to run toward Him, giving thanks for His forgiveness and continued love.

Sin always lies. It says, "Come my direction, and you will be better off with more pleasure and more satisfaction." It promises like a god but pays like the devil. We must never deny the fact that sin is pleasurable; however, that sinful pleasure turns to guilt and spiritual slavery. Moses, we are told, chose obedience to God rather than enjoying the "fleeting pleasures of sin" (Hebrews 11:25). Sinful pleasure lasts a short time, "a season," but then it's gone. The aftertaste continues.

Poet Robert Burns wrote:

But pleasures are like poppies spread,
You seize the flower, its bloom is shed;
Or like the snow falls in the river,
A moment white—then melts forever.[7]

When Abraham feared as the armies he had defeated were plotting against him, God said to him, "Fear not, Abram, I am your shield; your reward shall be very great" (Genesis 15:1). God was telling Abraham that He was with him and that he would have a great reward—which included a sense of rest, satisfaction, and gladness. That is why the Psalms are so filled with exhortations to rejoice in God. It is because God Himself rewards those who seek and rejoice in Him.

How Do We Seek God?

So, how do we seek God?

A word to those who have only thought of God as a slot machine; those who ask and ask but never seek His face; to a generation where prayer is primarily self-serving: How do we stop our selfishness and say to ourselves, "I want to seek God"? If God generously rewards those who seek Him, we want to be among those who take Him up on it. Do you want to seek God and receive His generous reward?

We Choose to Agree with God

Agreement begins with silence: Stop talking and demanding. The psalmist said, "My soul, wait silently for God alone, for my expectation is from Him" (Psalm 62:5 NKJV). The silence exposes your life and all the intents of your heart to a God who already sees you. And in your silence, you are living out a disposition—a willingness to receive, a willingness to be totally honest.

You are saying, "God, not only do You see me, but show me what You see so that I can deal with it. What are the stones that must be removed in my life in order to have a clear relationship with You? What is standing in the way?" This is known as confession. The word "confess" means to agree with God. It says, "God, I agree that bitterness is sin, I agree that this relationship I'm in is sinful. I agree that the anxieties that I'm bearing are sinful because I'm carrying what I'm not supposed to carry." In the silence, we come and we agree with God. Of course, we can speak, but we do it with total submission. The hypocrisy game in the presence of the Lord is over.

We Adore God

Choose to adore God. Begin to read the Psalms, and read God's

Word back to Him. Use a hymnal and read the words or sing it. (God will be glad to hear your heart even if you're out of tune!)

When Scott, the co-writer of this book, first got married, he realized he married someone with a different schedule. He would often wake up before his wife, Michal. Early in the morning, he would sneak away for time with the Lord before she arose. Their first home was a two-story rental, and his office was located directly above the bedroom. Because of this arrangement, he would often remind himself to meet with the Lord a little more quietly, but sometimes, he would not be quiet enough. On those "less quiet" days, he would descend from his office on the second floor and often find that the song he was singing to the Lord was also being sung by his wife in the room below. Their days started with worship.

The Lord has since blessed Scott and Michal with four children. During breakfast, they have a time of devotion with the children. While many songs of worship are played and sung in their home, they enjoy singing the old hymns at the breakfast table. Their children love music and regularly hum the "breakfast tunes" throughout the day. Some days, it is as if the sweetness of worship saturates the home.

I agree with Scott. I noticed that the songs we sing on Sunday oftentimes are in my mind during the week. I am personally watching less news than I used to and listening to more gospel music. But let's not merely save such adoration for Sundays and hope for the best for the rest of the week. If you want to adore God, be intentional, regular, and sacrificial with your time. As mentioned, use the Bible, along with a hymnal, songbook, or even a Spotify playlist. Then adore God! Even a walk or a drive to work can be a holy time of worship. Why do you think God allowed human beings to invent headphones?

I love those moments where I look to the face of God in adoration and say, "Jesus, the very thought of thee with sweetness fills the breast; but sweeter far thy face to see, and in thy presence rest."[8]

In adoration, you are reminding yourself of God and His attributes, but you are also reminding yourself of His relationship with you. You are building that relationship. Like a husband or a wife who rehearses the virtues of their spouse, the reminder confirms and builds the relationship. And remember, it's not about what you have done but what God has done!

We Affirm God's Love for Us

If you are a believer, God loves you with the same love He has for Jesus (John 17:22–25). But are you willing to let yourself believe that God loves you? You know yourself quite well—every thought and desire. You know you're unlovable. God should not love you. Whether you recognize it or not, that's true of all of us! The better we know ourselves, the more likely we want to say, "God, You really shouldn't love me."

The good news is that feelings are not facts; God loves us, and you are the object of His affection. You are number one on His list of things to take care of in this befuddled universe. Every hair of your head is numbered; He knows and cares for you so meticulously. Can you comprehend the particular interest God takes in His creation? Not even a sparrow falls to the ground without the heavenly Father's notice. He loves us so much that He gave that which was most precious to Him—His Son to suffer and die for us. Don't you dare say God doesn't love you!

In your time of prayer, do not forget to assure yourself that you're coming to a God who rejoices when you are in His presence. "He will rejoice over you with gladness; he will quiet you by his love" (Zephaniah 3:17). You have value because you are valuable to God. Jesus said, "Look at the birds of the air: they neither sow nor reap nor gather into barns, and yet your heavenly Father feeds them. Are you not of more value than they?" (Matthew 6:26). In Matthew 10:29–31, He reinforces the idea: "Are not two sparrows sold for a penny? And not one of them will fall to the ground apart from your Father. But even the hairs of your head are all numbered. Fear not, therefore; you are of more value than many sparrows."

God cares about you. He cares about whom you should marry (He also cares about whom you should *not* marry). Yes, He cares about your health and your relationships. Thank Him for it!

We Accept What God Has for Us

Now that seeking Him is your priority, ask of Him and let your requests be known, "Do not be anxious about anything, but in everything by prayer and supplication with thanksgiving let your requests be made known to God" (Philippians 4:6).

Thanksgiving precedes asking, and peace precedes understanding. A promise is given: "And the peace of God, which surpasses all understanding, will guard your hearts and your minds in Christ Jesus" (Philippians 4:7). Accept what God gives you.

Asking directly involves committing ourselves to God and surrendering our concerns to Him. Our concerns are completely in His hands. We make our requests, but we bring those requests and leave them submitted to the plan of God. We remember Jesus in Gethsemane: "Father, all things are possible for you. Remove this cup from me. Yet not what I will, but what you will" (Mark 14:36).

We Regularly Affirm Our Relationship

We've heard it said, "A chapter a day keeps the devil away." Not exactly! If you can't remember what you read after you finish reading it, what good will that Scripture be for you? Instead, as you read that chapter, look for a promise, look for an affirmation, look for a life-changing truth, and then put it into your mind for the rest of the day. Repeat it. Memorize it. Savor it. Set up camp with that verse and stay with it, focusing on that promise, affirmation, or truth.

You're now ready to enter the world. "Father, You know I must go to work. I have to get on the road. You know I must leave my knees and serve You in a different way as I go to my job or face this burden. Just know I do not desire to break fellowship with You. Father, please keep me in touch with You all day. . . . I am distracted, but I look to You for your intervention and help."

And throughout the day, we confess our sins as soon as we are aware of them.

Will you seek the Lord like this?

Perhaps you are wondering, "How much time should my morning routine take?" If I gave you a specific length of time, it would be one more legalistic thing to do—fulfilling your obligatory half hour, twenty minutes, or whatever. I would rather let you and God figure that out. Ask God how much time this should take. It's amazing how our heavenly Father can sometimes convey His will to a child who is willing to listen and respond.

Here's what you do. Take a small piece of paper or make a note in your phone and copy down these five steps from this chapter.

1. We choose to agree with God.
2. We adore God.
3. We affirm God's love for us.
4. We accept what God has for us.
5. We regularly affirm our relationship.

Save that note for when you pray. If it is on paper, stick it on the wall. You might even use it as a bookmark for your Bible as a reminder for each time you read and pray. And then let these five steps be a guide—and only a guide. Sometimes these steps might be interspersed or all in a row.

Most importantly, seek God! Why? The Bible says He rewards those who seek Him out. Seeking Him takes time and surrender, and it can be painful. But the reward is worth it!

Knowing God comes before asking God; and God's will comes before our will. This is essential.

"Seek the LORD while he may be found; call upon him while he is near; let the wicked forsake his way, and the unrighteous man his thoughts; let him return to the LORD, that he may have compassion on him, and to our God, for he will abundantly pardon" (Isaiah 55:6–7).

So, we have learned that *knowing* God comes before *asking* God; and *God's will* comes before *our will.* This is essential. And when God's will comes before ours, the whole purpose of prayer shifts.

Let's Get Started

Right now is the time to begin.

This verse has been quoted elsewhere in this book, but we cannot hear it too often: "We have confidence to enter the holy places by the blood of Jesus" (Hebrews 10:19). The text evokes the ancient temple to Yahweh with its sacred halls, including the holy of holies. Only priests could enter, and even then, God could strike down a sinful priest.

Brothers and sisters, you are right to hesitate in seeking God and entering His holy presence, but the text offers a way: through "the blood of Jesus." That is the way—the only way—you get to God: You acknowledge your sinfulness. You realize that Jesus Christ's blood was shed to take away the sin of sinners, offering the redemption and forgiveness you need. In Jesus, you can seek God.

Then you begin your journey of knowing God. And in a year from now, you'll look back and say, "I know God better than I did last year!"

Jeremiah 9:23–24 says:

> *Let not the wise man boast in his wisdom, let not the mighty man boast in his might, let not the rich man boast in his riches, but let him who boasts boast in this, that he understands and knows me, that I am the LORD who practices steadfast love, justice, and righteousness in the earth. For in these things I delight, declares the LORD.*

Let us pursue God and find our greatest joy is knowing Him!

A Prayer of Adoration

Do you know this old chorus? "Knowing you, Jesus; knowing you, there is no greater thing; You're my all, you're the best; You're my joy, my righteousness; and I love you, Lord."[9] As we seek God and know Him, adoration so swiftly follows.

If you have acknowledged your sin and trusted Christ, step one is to seek God. If you are in the midst of difficulty or if you lack the clarity you want from God, you can still praise God. Job did. "Blessed be the name of the Lord" (Job 1:21). Regardless of our feelings and circumstances, God is still the best, our joy, and our righteousness.

Praise to You, the magnificent One!

You have manifested Yourself to us.

You have redeemed us, the undeserving.

You have broken our bonds of iniquity!

You have wrought in us a desire for worship.

Praise, praise to the Savior!

Who quickened my lifeless soul (I was dead.)

Who saved me not according to merit (I had none.)

Who justified my condemned estate (Why me?)

Who credits unfathomable righteousness to His people (I deserve nothing.)

We acknowledge and adore You this day.

May Your name alone be glorified in me!

May Your honor be known among the nations!

May Your mercy be beheld by all!

May Your Spirit invoke a zeal in Your church for Your fame.

May it ever be so.

In Jesus' name, Amen.

Why Pray If God Is in Control?

Prayer does change things!

In C. S. Lewis's classic *The Screwtape Letters,* the fictional senior demon Screwtape is instructing his nephew Wormwood on how to be a "good" demon. Wormwood has been assigned to a person to ensure that the "patient" does not spiritually thrive. In Letter 27, Screwtape lectures Wormwood on how to undermine the person's prayer life. It seems that Wormwood cannot stop the prayers completely, so Screwtape makes this suggestion:

> *"You can worry him with the haunting suspicion that the practice [of prayer] is absurd and can have no objective result. Don't forget to use the 'heads I win, tails you lose' argument. If the thing he prays for doesn't happen, then that is one more proof that petitionary prayers don't work; if it does happen, he will, of course, be able to see some of the physical*

causes which led up to it, and 'therefore it would have happened anyway', and thus a granted prayer becomes just as good a proof as a denied one that prayers are ineffective."[1]

The scheme is straightforward. The demons of the story aim to win the battle regardless of what God does in response to the patient's prayers. If God does not answer, then Wormwood will lie to the man saying prayer is pointless. If God does answer, then Wormwood will lie that prayer is pointless because the answer to the prayer would have happened anyway.

"Why should I pray? God is going to do what God is going to do; my prayers will not affect His will. He will do His will, not my will!" That was the explanation of a man when I asked him why he didn't attend prayer meeting. In a single sentence, he basically said, "Since God is sovereign, our prayers don't matter." And if you have a list of unanswered prayers, that seems to be a reasonable conclusion.

Without the direct suggestion of a demon, have not all of us wondered, "Is prayer pointless? Doesn't God simply get His way regardless of how I pray? His will matters, not mine." It's a reasonable conclusion, but it's not a biblical one. In fact, Jesus didn't give us the option of thinking that prayer does not matter just because God is in control.

Let's ponder this: Jesus told His disciples they should not pray like the heathen who believe they will be heard because of their many words. And then He adds, "Do not be like them, for your Father knows what you need before you ask him" (Matthew 6:8). So, for all those skeptics who believe that prayer doesn't make a difference, there's your verse! God knows ahead of time what our needs are and how we are going to pray! So, why bother?

But Jesus doesn't allow us to go there. The very next words out of His mouth are "Pray then like this . . ." and He launches into what we call the Lord's Prayer. Of course, God knows our needs; of course, He already knows what we are going to ask for!

Jesus expects us to pray and to fast. One thing is very clear: We don't pray to inform God of anything! He never changes His mind because we give Him "new" information—He already knows all of the details. He's not like a politician who only responds when a great number of his constituents petition him.

The purpose of prayer is not to inform God, but to bring our thoughts and our will in line with His purposes.

The purpose of prayer is not to inform God, but to bring our thoughts and our will in line with His purposes. Prayer is God's invitation to join Him on what He intends to do in this world. We do not pray to overcome His reluctance but, as one person put it, we pray "to lay hold of His highest willingness."

Prayer might not change God, but it certainly changes us!

Let Us Embrace the Mystery

As we enter into this discussion of God's sovereignty let us never forget this: We pray and worship a God who responds to His people; we must ever come before Him and know that we come to welcoming God. Let not the mystery of God's ways deter us but draw us into His presence and enhance our worship and even enlarge our requests.

Yes, the interaction between human activity and God's sovereignty is a mystery, but it's one the Bible invites us to ponder. So, let's rehearse what we know about God, prayer, and how what we pray for does change things as James tells us.

The fact is, we do have examples in history and in the Bible where earnest prayer brought about a change of events. Elijah prayed, and drought came; he prayed again, and it rained. Moses prayed on the mountain, and God withdrew His threat to destroy the people; the early church prayed, and the place was "shaken," and they were given boldness to proclaim the gospel even to the point of death.

Revivals have come because of praying people; many wayward children have come to the Lord because the praying parents wouldn't take no for an answer. All of us can give testimony to the fact that, yes, God answers prayer. In prayer, God tests our desires, and we get to enter into His heart; by that I mean we get to know Him more intimately and trust Him more fully.

Let us pray for our needs individually and collectively as watchmen prayed for Jerusalem: "On your walls, O Jerusalem, I have set watchmen; all the day and all the night they shall never be silent. You who put the LORD in remembrance, take no rest, and give him [God] no rest until he establishes Jerusalem: and makes it a praise in the earth" (Isaiah 62:6–7).

Give God no rest!

I thank God for prayer ministries that seek to unite Christians in persistent, hopeful, and believing prayer. Prayerlessness in our lives is a sign that we have grown worldly in our thoughts and lifestyle. Too often we show our self-reliance and powerlessness, and I believe God would say to us, "You come to inform Me, but not to honor Me; you are coming to think you must overcome My reluctance but take no time to enter into what I am doing in the world. You come to use Me when you are in trouble, but not to enjoy My presence; you honor Me with your lips, but your heart is far from Me."

Let's continue to explore the mystery.

God Is in Control

From Genesis to Revelation, the Bible teaches that God works in and through all things. The natural order of creation, the weather, the sustaining of the animal kingdom: God takes credit for it all (see Job 38 and 39). Sun, rain, seasons, and rainbows come from His hand, with each ray of sunshine and drop of rain authored by God through creation-based systems like the hydrological cycle. We have already quoted the verse where Jesus says that the Father feeds the birds. His care for creation is comprehensive, and He maintains and utilizes natural systems to accomplish His sustaining work.

The natural order belongs to God; but does that meticulous control extend to the human mind? In Acts 17:26, we read that God "made from one man every nation of mankind to live on all the face of the earth, having determined allotted periods and the boundaries of their dwelling place." Job 12:23 tells us, "He [God] makes nations great, and he destroys them; he enlarges nations, and leads them away." The humbled King Nebuchadnezzar says that the Most High "does according to his will among the host of heaven and among the inhabitants of the earth; and none can stay his hand" (Daniel 4:35). The battles, the plagues, the movement of peoples—God oversees all of these and more.

This sovereignty of God extends to the human mind. Parents frequently pray for the salvation of their children or grandchildren without realizing they are asking God to intervene in the thought life of their child and that their stubborn will would be overcome by God's sovereign control. God is personally involved with each one of us!

This truth about God's sovereign control is precisely why we can lay down our head on our pillow at night. It is why Romans 8:28 means so much to many of us: "We know that for those who love God all things work together for good, for those who are called according to his purpose." This truth is why Ephesians 1:11 is such an encouragement! "In him we have obtained an inheritance, having been predestined according to the purpose of him who works all things according to the counsel of his will." Because God is working in and through all things (even when we cannot see it), our standing with God is sure no matter what this life may bring. *When* (not *if*) we encounter trials of various kinds, we can confidently rest in the knowledge that all things work together for our good.

We Are Making Authentic Decisions

God can do whatever He wants without our prayers, and yet we are involved in many things that He does. We must embrace the convergence of God's sovereignty and our responsibility. That is why Philippians 2:12 can command us to "work out your own salvation with fear and trembling," while also teaching that "it is God who works in you, both to will and to work for his good pleasure" (v. 13). In other words, we should strive to work in harmony with God; God works and so should we.

Think of it this way: God is the *ultimate* cause of everything that occurs, because without His oversight and sustenance, nothing would exist. But you are the *immediate* cause in your life's decisions. We make real decisions even as God orchestrates what we do.

To repeat: Embrace that mystery.

To deny the sovereignty of God is scary because it would

mean we believe in a God who is not in control of human events. (Could His promises be trusted?) And, conversely, asserting your independence from God's control is equally dangerous. Satan was the first one who desired to be independent from God. But even in rebellion, the evil one remains under God's authority until the appointed day for his doom.

Remember all of the wickedness done against Joseph? Yet he said to his brothers, "As for you, you meant evil against me, but God meant it for good, to bring it about that many people should be kept alive, as they are today" (Genesis 50:20). He doesn't just say that God took the evil of the brothers and used it for good, but rather that their evil was actually the fulfillment of God's plans.

The best illustration of this is the death of Jesus. He is crucified because of human action; however, the entire event was God's purpose (Acts 4:27–28). They were not *forced* to do what they did; they acted voluntarily. In other words, they did what they wanted to do; but behind their actions, God was directing events. People are responsible for their actions, even as God's purposes prevail.

God's sovereignty should not make us passive and lazy; it should give us courage. When we obey, we know God is working in us. When we preach the gospel, we acknowledge that God is reaching out to the lost. When seeking to fulfill God's stated will in the Bible, we can courageously move forward knowing God is working in and through us!

Obeying God's Commands

Prayer is not about getting our way like a spoiled child. His will prevails (see 1 John 5:14). Prayer is genuine communication with God Himself. And He has ordained prayer as a path to provision, fellowship, and participation.

And there is more to consider.

Frequently in Scripture, God gives people a burden to pray, and they become the means by which their prayers are fulfilled. Nehemiah had a burden to pray for the restoration of Jerusalem and ended up leading a delegation to rebuild the walls of Jerusalem; Jeremiah prayed that the Babylonian captivity would come to an end and in doing so, he was echoing God's will. When God wants to do something, He sets His people praying.

Through prayer, we get to join God in His work. In accordance with His plans, we pray and preach. He acts, transforming lives through the gospel in the power of the Spirit. Distant tribes would remain unreached by the gospel unless God lays it on the hearts of His children to pray. Wandering children would remain lost unless God gives them a godly parent who persists in prayer. God can do all these things and more whether we pray or not, but God invites us to enter into His work. As Paul put it, "You also must help us by prayer, so that many will give thanks on our behalf for the blessing granted us through the prayers of many" (2 Corinthians 1:11). He directly connects God's special blessing and the people's prayers.

Thanks to prayer, we can commune with God, dwelling together with Him. He is not like parents who insist that children must be "seen, not heard." No, He is a gracious Father who holds out His arms to us and calls us to Himself. We cannot inconvenience Him. Live with it: God is in control *and yet* our prayers matter!

Thanking God for Unanswered Prayers

Two male high school students were in love with the same young woman. Both young men loved the Lord and prayed extensively about this girl, asking God to play matchmaker. Both said, "God told me I will marry her." God in His wisdom, however, did not answer their request; in fact, neither of them married that girl. Probably the day came when both of them thanked God for not answering their prayer.

Have you ever considered the misguided and shortsighted prayers in the Bible? People were not always careful about their prayers. Abraham asked for Ishmael to be the heir of the promise (Genesis 17:18–21). That would likely have ended in centuries of disaster. Despite Samuel giving the Israelites numerous reasons not to seek a king, they still asked for one like all the other nations. And God consented.

We have the record of three separate prophets who were in such despair they asked God to end their lives. (You can read their prayers: Moses in Numbers 11:15; Elijah in 1 Kings 19:4; and Jonah in Jonah 4:1–8.) Thankfully, God didn't take them up on their requests. Of course, being a prophet is a tough job, but you can be reasonably confident that they didn't look favorably on those prayers later in life!

In 2007, Scott climbed Mt. Sinai. (I took the same trek back in 1969, before Scott was born!) The trek started in the rocky wilderness next to one of Christianity's oldest monasteries: St. Catherine's. But it was difficult to ascertain where the trail began since the ascent started off in the complete darkness of 3:00 a.m.

If you have summited a peak before, you know the struggle. Unless you're a seasoned climber, your legs ache. Your breathing is loud. You might occasionally stumble over a rock. Those experiences only worsen in the dark as you rush to the summit before sunrise. Plus, the Sinai path is wide enough that people hire camels to carry them up part of the way. An unseen camel's loud snort can shock a hiker.

By the time Scott finished the path and took the last 750 steps up the stone staircase to the peak, he was exhausted. And because it was dark, he still had no idea about the surprise he would experience. But the sun rose, and the Christian climbers burst into praise, singing hymns to the Lord as the light streamed over the barren peaks of the Egyptian wilderness. The exhaustion of the tough and discouraging climb gave way to relief, joy, and worship.

Often, we experience the same in our trials. We struggle. We pray. We suffer in the darkness, wondering why all of the pain is happening. We think about turning back. We want to quit. But then one day, God grants light, and like a climber watching the sunrise from the top of a majestic mountain, we finally see what He has done in us through our trials.

"Why doesn't God answer my prayers?" I don't know. But don't stop praying! The trial may not make sense now, but someday soon (either in this world or the next), you will see what God has done. Until that day, I don't know how difficult the journey is going to be for you. But may I offer some final words for the path ahead?

Respond to any burden God has laid on your heart, and even if you don't feel like praying, pray anyway! Begin praying biblical prayers. Even the martyrs in heaven pray:

> *When he opened the fifth seal, I saw under the altar the souls of those who had been slain for the word of God and for the witness they had borne. They cried out with a loud voice, "O Sovereign Lord, holy and true, how long before you will judge and avenge our blood on those who dwell on the earth?" Then they were each given a white robe and told to rest a little longer, until the number of their fellow servants and their brothers should be complete, who were to be killed as they themselves had been. (Revelation 6:9–11)*

Do not be afraid to use "how long" prayers: "*How long* will You let this trial continue? Will You withhold Your hand indefinitely? I choose to hope in You, trusting that Your assistance is not far off." In fact, "how long" prayers are the standard cry of the church itself. "How long before You return, Jesus?" And thus, at the end of the book of Revelation, the Spirit and God's people call out, "Come!" How much longer will we wait? Not long. May we yearn for His arrival!

Remember what we have learned earlier in this book. Your prayers may be unanswered, but they have been heard. So, a final word:

Never interpret the silence of God as the indifference of God.

A Prayer of Hope for the Coming World

As this book draws to a close, you may feel a bit melancholy, torn between despair and hope. On one hand, despair may persist because your problems remain. Your prayers have not been answered, and the road ahead may seem long and difficult. On the other hand, hope may have taken root in your heart. For once, your unanswered prayers have meaning. The complete fulfillment of God's promises toward you is near. If this is you, struggling with despair and hope, you have your hands full! With that challenge in mind, here is one last prayer for you.

May we begin to live in this world for the coming world—the eternal city. And soon, all despair will fade away at the coming of our King, and our hope shall be realized.

Eternal Father,

I live in the present. I walk in the world.

Too often, I live for the present
and walk with the world.

I long for the health of my body,
even as my soul withers.

I buy the world's goods, but somehow
worldly possessions own me.

The world promises freedom, but
all I receive is bondage.

The city of man guarantees "the good
life," but death is all I see.

Father,

Help me to follow Abraham to Your eternal city.

Grow spiritual life in this body of death, that
I may trust in Christ without reservation.

I want to live in the present, with hope in the future.

I want to walk in the world, without a love for it.

Swallow up my lesser loves with a love for You.

I choose to love You even when
tragedy and trial prevail.

And may I extend love to those ensnared
by a world that is passing away.

I pray with hope, until the eternal city is revealed.

In Jesus' name, Amen.

Appendix: Prayers for "Stuck" People

In this book, we've learned about people who feel stuck in their relationship with God. "Stuck" people are dealing with a pressing challenge and believe God is still saying no. Discouragement rises. Prayer becomes repetitive, one-dimensional, and even demanding. The trial becomes all-consuming, and one's prayer life revolves around that trial.

When I'm stuck, I find that a prayer book can be a helpful tool because it leads me to pray something different. Here is a portion of one of my favorite prayers from *The Valley of Vision*. You can take a moment to pray it now.

> *Father,*
> *I am well pleased with your will, whatever it is,*
> *or should be in all respects,*
> *And if you bid me to decide for myself in any affair,*
> *I would choose to refer all to you,*
> *for you are infinitely wise and cannot do wrong,*

as I am in danger of doing.
I rejoice to think that all things are at your disposal,
and it delights me to leave them there.
Then prayer turns wholly into praise,
and all I can do is to adore and bless you.
Amen.[1]

A prayer book is not about reciting magic words, line by line. It is a jumping-off point for times and subjects of prayer you might not find on your own, especially if you're stuck. Here are some books that you might find helpful:

- *A Journey to Victorious Praying: Finding Discipline and Delight in Your Prayer Life* (Bill Thrasher)
- *A Passion for Prayer* (Tom Elliff)
- *Be Thou My Vision: A Liturgy for Daily Worship* (Jonathan Gibson)
- *Fount of Heaven: Prayers of the Early Church* (ed. Robert Elmer)
- *Handbook to Prayer: Praying Scripture Back to God* (Kenneth Boa)
- *Heart of God: 31 Days to Discover God's Love for You* (Elisabeth Elliot)
- *Prayers of Rest* (Asheritah Ciuciu)
- *The Valley of Vision: A Collection of Puritan Prayers and Devotions* (ed. Arthur G. Bennett)

Many more books could be listed. But in addition to these recommendations, Scott and I want to include some of our prayers—two weeks' worth to be exact. If you are stuck, it is our prayer that you may find rest in seeking your Lord in a different way.

A Prayer for Hope When God Appears to Turn Against Us

Poor Job. He loses everything and encounters a silent heaven. Yet the constant accusations of his friends drone on. Job bursts out in a soliloquy revealing his abandonment and despair. And yet, he is not without hope. Burdened with bitterness and frustration, he laments that he is unable to find God no matter how sincere or desperate his search. Somehow, he cleaves to his faith in God and says, "But he knows the way that I take; when he has tried me, I shall come out as gold" (Job 23:10).

Pray that prayer for yourself or someone who has abandoned their faith because of the apparent indifference of God. Be honest in your disappointment with God's perceived lack of concern, but also rejoice that He will bring us through, stronger than ever, because "the tested genuineness of your faith—more precious than gold that perishes though it is tested by fire—may be found to result in praise and glory and honor at the revelation of Jesus Christ" (1 Peter 1:7).

Father,

I confess that I have been disappointed because it appears You have not answered my prayers and cries for help. Today, my need is great and specific, and I bring it to You again. Lord, help me to be content in difficulty and suffering.

I recall Your Word, "For your sake we are being killed all the day long; we are regarded as sheep to be slaughtered" (Romans 8:36).

I choose to persevere for Your sake.

Assure me that hardship is not Your abandonment of me.

Remind me of Your faithfulness.

I pray that I might say with Job, "Though he slay me, I will hope in him" (Job 13:15).

When I doubt, give me hope.

When I am in despair, give me comfort.

Let not accusers hinder me from believing in Your goodness and provision. Instead, let grace and peace overwhelm me. Today, reveal Yourself to me that I may pass this test of apparent abandonment and know that You are close to me, even in my trials and disappointment.

In Jesus' name, Amen.

A Prayer for Worship in Trial

Back to Job again. God finally speaks, and He does not deliver a word of comfort. Instead, He asks Job at least two dozen questions He knows Job can't answer. God's point stings a bit: If you don't understand the created, physical realm, what makes you think you can understand what I'm doing beyond your sight? In a way, God is saying, "Job, what makes you think you can understand My purposes for you or anyone else?"

The encounter humbles Job. He was passing judgment on the Almighty, calling into question His justice and care for one of His servants. Now that he has an opportunity to speak, he replies, "Behold, I am of small account; what shall I answer you? I lay my hand on my mouth" (Job 40:4). Having encountered God, he now realizes that God's wisdom and justice are beyond human understanding.

In the presence of God, only one proper response exists: worship. And, as Job learned, we can worship God even without explanations.

Pray that all of us would be more consistent in our worship, knowing God is beyond our understanding. If we could "find Him out" and discern His hidden purposes, we would be bringing Him down to our level. Before you pray, pause and read Job 42:1–6.

Father,

I worship You today.

I confess that I have complained against You because life is often difficult for no apparent reason.

I have questioned Your ways, believing that if I had Your power, I would have done a better job of running this universe than You.

I repent of such arrogance and selfishness before You, my Creator and Redeemer.

Father, I pray for myself, my family, and my friends that they may not rebel against Your sovereignty.

When they see injustice in the world, may they refuse to ascribe it to You.

May they remember that You, O Lord, are God, and we are not.

Help them to believe that Your way is perfect, and let that admission lead to submission, repentance, and thanksgiving.

In Jesus' name, Amen.

A Prayer That We Might Believe God During Tragedy

I (Erwin) can't forget the Haitian earthquake of 2010. It killed nearly 200,000 people, and one news interview is still vivid in my mind. A reporter was interviewing a young mother with a baby in her arms.

She said, "I lost my son. He died in the rubble."

The reporter asked, "Did you get to bury him?"

"No, no chance. His body was crushed in the rubble. I just had to throw him away."

Then the camera zeroed in on her backpack as she prepared to board a bus. A Bible was visible, sticking out of a side pocket of the backpack. As she boarded the bus, the interview was over. The camera lingered, and she began speaking to no one in particular. "God is our refuge and strength, an ever-present help in trouble . . ." Her voice trailed off as she disappeared from view.

When the report was over, I kept staring at the television for a moment, pushing back tears and letting what I had seen sink into my soul. This dear woman had lost a son. She had a baby in her arms. And because of the earthquake, she was boarding a bus to live who knows where.

Somehow, she was still believing, still trusting that God is her refuge and strength.

She was quoting Psalm 46, a praise song for when God spared the city of Jerusalem during the invasion of the Assyrians. God granted a harrowing escape for His people, and they found God as their unshakable pillar. Please read the entire Psalm for yourself.

Let us pray for all those who are experiencing calamities. Let us also pray for ourselves that we would be able to trust God even when it does not make sense, humanly speaking.

Father,

May I have the faith to trust You even when I experience devastating loss—whether it be my child, my home, or my job.

Grant me the faith to believe that I belong to You and You belong to me.

Even when my life in this world is filled with loss, remind me that this time is short and eternity is long.

God be a comfort to __________ that they might trust You amid their loss.

When their faith fails, strengthen them to believe that Your promises are still true.

May they remember that Your care for them is not defined by prosperity in this world, but by Your safeguarding of them to their heavenly home.

Strengthen our faith for we are weak.

In Jesus' name, Amen.

A Prayer for Faith in a Desperate Moment

Imagine being responsible not only for your own fate, but also the fate of a nation. Jehoshaphat found himself in such a predicament. A great army was moving against the land of Judah. Filled with fear, he "set his face to seek the LORD" (2 Chronicles 20:3) and called the people together to fast and pray for God's mercy and protection.

He prayed earnestly, confessing his sin and the sin of his people, reminding himself of God's greatness and the covenant with Israel. Listen to some of his words of desperation: "O our God, will you not execute judgment on them? For we are powerless against this great horde that is coming against us. We do not know what to do, but our eyes are on you" (2 Chronicles 20:12).

Jehoshaphat understood that he was no match for the overwhelming superiority of the invading armies. For deliverance to be possible, God had to directly intervene.

This prayer of desperation was also accompanied with worship. "Then Jehoshaphat bowed his head with his face to the ground, and all Judah and the inhabitants of Jerusalem fell down before the LORD, worshiping the LORD" (20:18). Next, Jehoshaphat turned military strategy on its head by sending a choir ahead of his own army! Should we be surprised when we read, "And when they began to sing and praise, the LORD set an ambush against the men of Ammon, Moab, and Mount Seir, who had come against Judah, so that they were routed" (20:22).

Do you detect the lessons for us when we are in a desperate moment? First, God can use whatever means He wishes to deliver us. He can thwart armies and reverse whatever seems to be coming at us. He is never in need of ideas to deliver us. Second, God answers when we ask in faith—a faith fueled by worship. One of the best things we can do when we're in a frightful place is to pause and give praise to God with singing and the affirmation of His promises. Desperate praying unaccompanied with praise is almost always a prayer of unbelief. Praise captures God's ear, and He responds, though not always in the way we expect.

Father,

Teach me to praise You at all times, especially when I am confronted by my enemies.

I have deep-seated fears within my soul about my future, my health, and especially about those whose greatest delight would be to witness my destruction.

Lord, today I turn away from those fears to give You praise.

Like the choir that led the armies of Judah into battle, I move forward with praise and gratitude for Your great name and the power of Your love.

I pray for my family and friends that they might develop the habit of giving You praise each morning.

May they read the psalms of praise, giving You their thanks and worship.

Teach them even as You teach me, that when we do not know what to do, praise is always the right response.

Together may we quote the words of Jehoshaphat's choir, "Give thanks to the Lord, *for his steadfast love endures forever" (2 Chronicles 20:21).*

Let Your praise be continually on our lips.

In Jesus' name, Amen.

A Prayer for God's Nearness—and Confession

The Lord has repeatedly demonstrated His expectations for complete purity among His people. In the Old Testament, God judged the rebellion of Korah with overwhelming force (Numbers 16). In the New Testament, the Holy Spirit ended the lives of Ananias and Sapphira for their deception (Acts 5:1–11).

Friends, God has not changed. The God who judged Korah and Ananias is the same God we worship today. The wages of sin are still death, and He reserves the right to hand us our paycheck when He sees fit.

Are you prepared for the God who comes near? He is not far off. He purifies His people, and that demands refinement and purification. He comes to bring light, exposing your sin, but will it not hurt when He scrubs your soul's every crevice? David invites Him in Psalm 139:23, "Search me, O God, and know my heart! Try me and know my thoughts!"

As you kneel to pray today, the Holy One is already present. Read and pray Psalm 139 to Him. Like David who cried "search me," let us welcome His work.

O Holy One,

I welcome Your presence today, like when a candle enters the darkness.

Come alongside Your servant, search me, and expose my flaws.

By Your nearness, destroy every vestige of self-righteousness.

Convict me of every sinful desire and misplaced word,

May Your holiness be reflected throughout my being.

Fill me with sanctifying truth! Make me holy as You are holy.

By the Holy Spirit's discipline, end my sins.

You are here, with me in my filth.

I am revolted by my sins and frightened by You—the Holy One.

Change me.

In Jesus' name, Amen.

A Prayer to Confess the Sinfulness of Our Prayers

Prayer reflects our heart. The two men praying in Luke 18 are a perfect example of this truth. Both pray! But the Pharisee's heart is filled with pride while the tax collector's heart is filled with humility.

Have you ever taken stock of a Bible study or a church's prayer time? If you listen carefully, you can detect where the community's priorities lie. Various types of prayer such as worship, submission, provision, reconciliation, and protection can go missing. While praying for the sick is important, sometimes that's all God's people do.

Often our holy avenue of approaching our loving Father is regularly tainted by our selfish, idolatrous proclivities. Prayer is so often about us and what we want, not God and His kingdom. Like a self-important toddler, we ask favors of our Father while not submitting to Him.

After meditating on Luke 18:9–14, let us confess the sinfulness of our prayers.

Lord of my salvation, God of constant provision,

Turn Your gaze toward me,

Show Your face to me.

I am but a wretch who begs before You.

I bask, bloated with Your many gifts,
yet I am often vacant of gratitude.

Forgive and dispel my foolish and selfish wantings.

I am but soul and flesh, corrupted
thoroughly from within.

Even my righteous desires are polluted in
prayer, as I stir in my own selfish aims.

My pleas themselves are held
hostage by my iniquities.

Set me free from the slavery to self.

Purify my thoughts and grant me holy
prayers marked by humility and worship.

Recognizing the shortcomings of my prayers,
provide me with what I do not perceive to
request, even what I do not want to ask.

In Jesus' name, Amen.

A Warfare Prayer Against the Powers

When we decide to fight our selfishness and say to God "Your kingdom come," we should expect evil's allies to reinforce our flesh's cause. The patterns of this wicked world and the demonic powers around us will seek to strengthen the hand of sin which grips our hearts.

We are often blind to the cosmic nature of our struggle in this flesh and in this world. We naturally acquiesce to the dominant ideas, practices, and routines of our cultures and countries. "Everybody is doing it." "Everybody thinks this way." Animated and controlled by "the god of the age" (Satan), many of our customs and philosophies are contrary to the one true God over the ages.

But because of Christ, we can finally see. Colossians 2:13–15 says:

> And you, who were dead in your trespasses and the uncircumcision of your flesh, God made alive together with him, having forgiven us all our trespasses, by canceling the record of debt that stood against us with its legal demands. This he set aside, nailing it to the cross. He disarmed the rulers and authorities and put them to open shame, by triumphing over them in him.

The powers are disarmed, unmasked, and "put to open shame." Jesus exposes the demonic deceptions that control the nations. And the gospel truth strides boldly among the lies of our time, striking down their hold on humanity. Today, let us join the battle. The war is within and without. Let us march with Christ.

Lord, You who conquers the powers,

I am a citizen of Your everlasting kingdom.

Philosophies of the age are rendered
foolish by the cross I claim.

Parties and politics are temporary institutions
unable to win the war I wage.

Principalities and powers are beneath the Christ-won
throne where I abide (Ephesians 1:20–23; 2:6).

Yet the cosmic forces—those rebellious beings
of unseen realm—still manipulate me.

I love to be eloquent in worldly wisdom, rather
than be identified with the cross's shame.

I campaign more for political wins
than for spiritual victories.

I quickly submit to my old guardians,
the powers that once ruled me.

Christ, You have unmasked the powers!

I see that the nations have been misled,

Seduced by the "no gods" of false religion
who dictate our days and devotions,

Marred by cultural corruptions that
obscure the law of conscience.

Fooled to pursue redemption and meaning in
personal effort, politics, and impure sacrifice.

I praise You, King of kings.

The demons shudder. The princes tremble.
The world shakes, for the King has come.

The truth has been revealed:

Dagon is fallen; the gods are weak.

Demons plead for mercy; the legion is disarmed.

Deliverance draws near; the serpent
writhes under the Nazarene sandal.

Lord, I am a haven of your Spirit,

Illumined by His truth, led by His guidance,

Reformed by His discipline, secured by His seal,

Yet my heart's wiles whisper like a demon.

Unchecked, I would yet seek to serve the dark
host, the world powers with which I struggle.

Within and without, the conflict rages:

My inner nature still seethes with Satan's rebellion,

My family still passes down the
philosophies of the powers,

My people still perpetuate revolt and
rebellion against You, the Lord.

O Blessed Spirit of God, help me to
adopt a singular allegiance,

Persevering when I am ostracized by
human relations of blood and anthem,

Resilient when I am oppressed
by demonic harassment,

Joyful when I lose my life, my job,
my access to worldly dreams.

Crush the enemy; uproot his rule.

Seat me with You; set my mind above.

In Jesus' name, Amen.

A Prayer for Better Emotions

Some of us grew up hearing that being emotional was a bad thing. In a sense, it's true; being controlled by anger and anxiety is not good! But emotions are not inherently evil. Jesus had emotions, and in Him, we see that holiness does not equal stoicism and emotionlessness.

Emotions are not supposed to be expunged; they're to be purified. In our natural state, emotions are contorted and controlled by our flesh. Even among the redeemed, our emotions fail us. The sorrows we feel are worldly. The anger we exhibit is murderous rather than righteous. The loves we share are reciprocal and deficient of self-sacrifice. The holy affections prescribed in Scripture and modeled by Christ are rendered unfeeling by our callousness and apathy.

Consider 1 Peter 4:7–8. The apostle says, "The end of all things is at hand; therefore be self-controlled and sober-minded for the sake of your prayers." But the text does not end there. Peter continues, "Above all, keep loving one another earnestly, since love covers a multitude of sins." We are commanded to live with self-control and sober-mindedness, denying our passions. Yet, we can pursue a life of true affection—the love modeled by God Himself. Today, let us die to the old way of emoting, and partake in the affections of God.

Father God,

I confess that my emotions are controlled by my flesh. Grant me true sorrow. Instead of sorrowing over my losses in this world, would You provoke in me a deep pain for the perishing, the unreached? I want to yearn for the lost, those who do not know Your name.

Grant me true anger. I am too often given to rage, bitterness, and hate because of the things of this world. Would You stir up in me a holy jealousy for Your fame? I want to burn when so-called Christians misrepresent You, maligning You and Your Word. May this zealousness strengthen my legs to stand for the truth.

Grant me true love. While the world wishes to enthrall me with lesser loves of romance and loving those who love me, I want to love like You. Would You instigate in me a longing to give my life away for those who can never repay me?

In You, because of You, and for You, I ask for true sorrow, anger, and love.

Help me, Your child.

In Jesus' name, Amen.

A Prayer for the Father's Discipline

The zeitgeist, the "spirit of the age," circulates a counterfeit love, often as a cover for sin. The love on offer today is the blind acceptance of the behaviors of others with no regard for the morality they exhibit. Everyone does what is right in their own eyes. Refusing to disturb that order and affirming that arrangement is deemed love.

God's love is not so feckless. With His good and immutable character as the backdrop, He loves us and changes us. Like a wise Father, He disciplines us that we might reflect His qualities in the world, just as He intended humanity to do from the beginning. Hebrews 12:7–11 says:

> It is for discipline that you have to endure. God is treating you as sons. For what son is there whom his father does not discipline? If you are left without discipline, in which all have participated, then you are illegitimate children and not sons. Besides this, we have had earthly fathers who disciplined us and we respected them. Shall we not much more be subject to the Father of spirits and live? For they disciplined us for a short time as it seemed best to them, but he disciplines us for our good, that we may share his holiness. For the moment all discipline seems painful rather than pleasant, but later

it yields the peaceful fruit of righteousness
to those who have been trained by it.

He cares for us. He acts so that we can share in His holiness. Encounter true love in God's discipline.

Father of unending compassion,

You deserve glory, adoration, and devotion!

But no child of yours, including me,
consistently bestows this to You.

I am a sinner. I stray. I wander. I have set up idols of worthless things and sadly misplaced my affections. I disobey. I fail to do what is right. I do what is right with bad motives and a poor attitude.

Do not stand by when I have need of my good Father. Keep me from my potential sins, and drive me from my current sins.

Father, Your compassion is unfailing.

You will not let me sin without recompense.

Your infinite love leads to divine discipline.

I accept Your chastisement.

Lead me again and again to my knees.

In Jesus' name, Amen.

A Prayer for a Mind Completely Focused on God

God is not the problem. We are. We fall short. He does not. The divine mind is not in tension, division, or frustration. Meanwhile, sin has caused human disintegration on an unfathomable scale. The human mind is corrupted, not God's.

Our right desires, our pursuit of relationship, our religious activities—we imbue each one with duplicitous schemes. Jesus warns us, "Beware of practicing your righteousness before other people in order to be seen by them, for then you will have no reward from your Father who is in heaven" (Matthew 6:1). Our prayers are so easily tainted. Yet the Spirit cries out to us, that we may live in simplicity and unity of mind before God.

We must stop being double-minded. Let us renounce the hypocrisy that taints and stains our every thought and deed lest we outwardly ally with Christ while covertly gratifying the flesh and supporting the enemy.

Spend time in Matthew 6 and then let us pray together.

Immutable God,

Restore my disintegrated mind, for I am fractured by indwelling sin, longing to exemplify the cross yet selfishly gratifying the flesh.

Often do I claim Christ only with my lips,

Behave biblically for self-glory,

Attend church only for social ends,

Pursue holiness with a competitive spirit.

Though redeemed through faith in Christ,

Which shelters my soul from wrath, which grants everlasting righteousness,

Which relieves sin's condemnation, which beckons me to godly living;

My sinful desires are many.

Unchanging Father,

Unite my mind that I may be

Wholly following the guidance of the Spirit of the Holy,

Completely imitating the attitude of Christ.

In Jesus' name, Amen.

A Prayer for Attentiveness to God

When a child discovers a new toy—a doll, a ball, or even an interesting stick—the rest of the world fades from their sight. They lock their gaze, focusing their attention on nothing else. And if you are a parent, you probably know the challenge of tearing them away from that toy. You must repeat the child's name before they snap back into reality.

What has arrested your vision in this world? Binge watching shows is one common example. Someone finds a new series, then their whole week's schedule revolves around when they will be able to watch the next episode. While it may not be a show, what has drawn your attention, crowding out all competitors—whether they be worthy or worthless?

Whatever draws your gaze, it has probably sidelined the theme of redemption. The Scriptures reflect that the Father, Son, and Spirit are wholly interested in the redemption of humanity, yet we rarely are engrossed by the wonders of salvation—purchased in the past, applied in the present, concluded in the future. Let us return to the glories of redemption and reflect deeply.

Take a moment to slowly read through Ephesians 1 before you pray.

Jesus,

Rescue me!

You are the Redeemer King,

Who purchased me as a possession out of the nations,

Who restored my life through an excruciating death,

Who walked without wrong in a wicked world,

Who stained the earth with blameless blood to cleanse hearts.

Rescue me!

You are the One who redeems still,

Who reminds me of His personal ownership over my estate,

Who provides abundantly for every need and worry,

Who grants the Spirit that holiness may increase,

Who illumines my daily path of following You, denying myself, and carrying my cross.

Rescue me,

From my ignorant eyes and my narrow vision.

I look to You today.

In Jesus' name, Amen.

A Prayer in the Paradoxical Path

God's purposes are somehow revealed, yet still paradoxical. Even the most devout Christian can still feel bewildered, wondering why God's children suffer so much in this world. Let us to look to Jesus afresh today. According to the will of God, the exalted Son of God came to us. Yet His route to resurrection and glory involved starving (fasting for forty days qualifies in my book), suffering (even before the cross), studying Scripture (as He grew up), foot-washing (like a servant), forgiving (friends and enemies), and resisting temptation (after starving). That is a path of humility. Why did He have to suffer so much in this world?

God's purposes extend to us, including suffering, whether it finds us in persecution or we find it in fasting. This is the paradoxical path of God: His people would accomplish much by being little in this world. In the words of Arthur Bennett:

> Let me learn by paradox that the way down is the way up,
> that to be low is to be high,
> that the broken heart is the healed heart,
> that the contrite spirit is the rejoicing spirit,
> that the repenting soul is the victorious soul,
> that to have nothing is to possess all,
> that to bear the cross is to wear the crown.[2]

The world will never understand the paradox, but as children of God, we can by faith. Let us follow Jesus in His humility until the day that the Father raises us to glory.

Meditate on 1 Peter 2:20–21. "For what credit is it if, when you sin and are beaten for it, you endure? But if when you do good and suffer for it you endure, this is a gracious thing in the sight of God. For to this you have been called, because Christ also suffered for you, leaving you an example, so that you might follow in his steps." Let us pray.

Lord of hidden purposes,

Thank You that Your Son shows me that I can live with humility as I follow You.

Will You help me to offer humble prayers by keeping my focus on You?

To ascend to a heavenly perspective by descending to my knees,

To stand boldly before all by sitting in private meditation,

To devour the fruit of the Spirit by fasting from the fruit of the earth,

To lead among the rulers by living as a servant,

To live eternally by dying daily?

Remind me to crush sinful behaviors by constructing holy habits,

To dismiss demonic doctrines by receiving the Spirit's instruction,

To release selfishness by clinging to selflessness,

To withdraw from shame by approaching the cross,

To forget others' wrongs by
remembering Your forgiveness,

To ignore the world's temptations by
acknowledging Christ's freedoms.

Help this weary servant, for Your glory's sake.

May I follow You into suffering, trusting
that everlasting glory is coming.

According to Jesus' example and
in Jesus' name, Amen.

A Prayer to Be Like Our Master

Are we servants who are greater than the Master? If we remember Matthew 10:24, we instinctively respond "No, of course not!" But by the way we pray and the contents of those prayers, we betray our self-seeking attitude. We expect God to give us a life that looks very little like Christ's. We presume ourselves to be disciples who don't have to face any of the challenges of the biblical disciples!

Grief, sorrow, and rejection were with Jesus constantly. He was treated poorly by His human family. Some of you know that feeling all too well. And many Christian converts around the world are completely abandoned by their loved ones. Jesus knew that grief. But more than that, Jesus' heavenly Father crushed Him. Isaiah 53:4–6, 10–11 says:

> Surely he [the Messiah, Jesus] has borne our griefs and carried our sorrows; yet we esteemed him stricken, smitten by God, and afflicted. But he was pierced for our transgressions; he was crushed for our iniquities; upon him was the chastisement that brought us peace, and with his wounds we are healed. All we like sheep have gone astray; we have turned—every one—to his own way; and the LORD has laid on him the iniquity of us all . . . Yet it was the will of the LORD to crush him; he has put him to grief; when his soul

> makes an offering for guilt, he shall see his offspring; he shall prolong his days; the will of the LORD shall prosper in his hand. Out of the anguish of his soul he shall see and be satisfied; by his knowledge shall the righteous one, my servant, make many to be accounted righteous, and he shall bear their iniquities.

According to the will of God, the Father crushed His Son. Can you imagine the possibility where being crushed and afflicted fulfills the purposes of God? Can you imagine such a possibility? Many people can't fathom the idea that God would want to crush them. If you can't see how your heavenly Father could do such a thing to you, then admit it: You think you're a servant who is greater than your Master.

Heavenly Father,

Thank You for Your gracious will to redeem
me through the sacrifice of Your Son.

Extend to me Your wisdom, which
You offer from Your abundance.

In these trying times where I fight to
focus, long to care, hope for holiness;

Guide me, by Your wisdom, not mine.

Tear me, then mend me anew.

Crush me, then build me up.

For Your glory, mold me and change me,

To be like Your Son, prepared to do
Your will, no matter the cost.

In Jesus' name, Amen.

A Prayer for Better Prayer

Prayer is the privilege of God's people. In prayer, our Father hears us, communes with us, and prepares us for His purposes. Just as prayer nourishes us in our private moments with God, prayer also revitalizes and mobilizes the corporate gathering of the church.

I hope you are praying with others. Pray together with your church, your family, your friends. Start a prayer group, and see what God does when His people pray together for His glory, kingdom, and will.

Some people are slow to pray in groups. They quote Matthew 6:5–6 to support their solitary prayer life:

> And when you pray, you must not be like the hypocrites. For they love to stand and pray in the synagogues and at the street corners, that they may be seen by others. Truly, I say to you, they have received their reward. But when you pray, go into your room and shut the door and pray to your Father who is in secret. And your Father who sees in secret will reward you.

I don't think Jesus is prohibiting public prayer in this passage; rather He is rebuking showmanship and providing a straightforward remedy for it.

Jesus is on to something. We can so easily corrupt prayer—whether it is public or private. Christians are recovering sin addicts, and hindrances and temptations abound both in church meetings and prayer closets. We need to pray for better prayer.

Father,

Ward off everything that hinders my communication with You, especially timidity and pride.

Provoke me to pray—

Individually with consistency and secrecy,

Corporately with courage and fervency.

Utilize every means,

Whether by good or ill, by health or pain, by wealth or lack, by presence or absence,

To demand my prayers.

May I not grow quiet.

Father,

When I am alone in prayer,

Wash away my self-righteousness from godly obedience,

Wash away my callousness from faithful recurrence,

Wash away my restlessness from holy stillness,

Wash away my timidity from heavenly humility,

That I may speak with You, my Master and friend.

Father,

When I am united with Your people in prayer,

Challenge us to offer bold requests,

Challenge us to lift wholehearted thanks,

Challenge us to display an unwavering voice, not given to fear,

Challenge us to have a hearing heart,

That we may pray as one for Your kingdom to come.

Father,

Why do our churches forget public prayer?

Why do we hide amid adorned walls to pray for the world?

Drive prayer to the streets for the hurt,

to the schools for the lost,

to the internet for the addicted,

May we pray at all times in all places, seeking the good of all.

Father,

Why does my mind wander when I pray? Where do my priorities lie?

Why do I turn to my own thoughts instead of turning to You?

I confess that I have too often abandoned private prayer.

I have ignored You, my own Father.

Steal me from my attention to cluttered schedules.

*Steal me from my affection to
degrading entertainment.*

Steal me from my associations with fruitless company.

Steal me from my fondness of iniquity,

May I pray consistently and constantly.

Father,

*Why do my feet wander from prayer?
Where would I rather be?*

*Why do I busy myself with selfish activities
instead of resting with You?*

Occupied by foe or friend, by work or pleasure,

May I obediently sequester myself with You.

As you beckon me to Yourself in prayer,

Overlook my shortcomings!

*I often pray with pagan repetition, as if You
do not hear and recognize my needs.*

*I often pray with reciprocal motives, as if You
will repay blessing for eloquent words.*

*I often pray with a controlling will, as if
You could be manipulated by me.*

*I often pray with a pharisaical spirit, as if
You do not notice my exhibitionism.*

Accept my wavering hands!

Acknowledge my fumbled words!

Redeem my inadequate prayers!

May Your Spirit convey my intentions
and cleanse my requests.

I long to pray better prayers.

In Jesus' name, Amen.

Acknowledgments

A book is never a solo project but takes a team. First of all, I (Erwin) want to pay tribute to Micah Shumate the Director of Moody Church Media. This book was his idea, and he and his team helped it becoming a reality. I remember the day he called me to say he had a project for me! Thanks, Micah, for your vision, persistence, and expertise in all you do. And soon John and Letricia were involved "making the rough places plain!"

Scott MacDonald, my co-writer, provided helpful content and wrote the prayers for the end of each chapter, which I know will be of great benefit to the readers in responding to what they have just read. Thanks, Scott, and I know you have a writing career ahead of you!

Of course, thanks to the Moody Publishers' team who carefully supervised this project right from the beginning. To you, Randall, publisher; Drew, acquisitions editor; Amanda, senior development editor: Thank you all so much for paying close attention to the process of bringing this book to completion. And I know that you are surrounded by many others equally devoted to getting gospel literature throughout the world.

Finally, and most importantly, I pay tribute to my lovely wife, Rebecca, to whom I have had the privilvege of being married for fifty-six years. Thanks, my love, for joining me on a long and winding journey, always at my side, always sacrificing for others, and always quick with your Soli Dei Gloria.

Erwin W. Lutzer

Notes

Chapter 1: Claiming Promises God Did Not Make

1. See D. R. McConnell, *A Different Gospel* (Hendrickson, 2004), 29–54.
2. For an overview of the history and doctrine of the Christian Science movement, please consult Walter Martin, *The Kingdom of the Cults* (Bethany House, 2003), 148–91.
3. "Is the Word of Faith Movement Biblical?," GotQuestions.org, https://www.gotquestions.org/Word-Faith.html.
4. Kris Vallotton, "How to Pray Prayers That Shape History," Kris Vallotton, https://podcast.krisvallotton.com/how-to-pray-prayers-that-shape-history.

Chapter 2: When You Pray, "Lord *Help* Me! But Don't *Change* Me!"

1. D. L. Moody, *Prevailing Prayer* (Moody, 2016), 125.

Chapter 3: When the Answer Is *Yes* but Not What You Expected

1. Athanasius, *The Life of Antony*, in *A Select Library of Nicene and Post-Nicene Fathers of the Christian Church*, Second Series, vol. 4, ed. Philip Schaff and Henry Wace, trans. H. Ellershaw (Hendrickson, 2004), 210–11.

Chapter 4: When a Prayer for Peace Ends in a National Disaster

1. John Piper, "Depression Fought Hard to Have Him," Desiring God, November 26, 2019, https://www.desiringgod.org/articles/depression-fought-hard-to-have-him.
2. William Cowper, "Sometimes a Light Surprises," Hymnal.net, https://www.hymnal.net/en/hymn/h/706.

Chapter 5: When the Request Is Denied

1. John MacArthur, "How God Uses Suffering, Part 1," Grace to You, February 1, 1998, https://www.gty.org/sermons/47-83/how-god-uses-suffering-part-1.
2. Dr. Howard Taylor, Geraldine Taylor, *Hudson Taylor's Spiritual Secret* (Moody, 2009), 165,
3. Taylor, *Hudson Taylor's Spiritual Secret*, 165,

Chapter 6: God in the Garden

1. C. S. Lewis, *Letters of C. S. Lewis*, ed. W. H. Lewis and Walter Hooper (Harcourt Books, 1993) 305.
2. Jonathan Edwards, "Christ's Agony," CCEL, https://www.ccel.org/ccel/edwards/sermons.agony.html.
3. Anne Ross Cousin, "O Christ, What Burdens Bow'd Thy Head!," Hymnal.net, https://www.hymnal.net/en/hymn/h/94.
4. Craig Keener, *The IVP Bible Background Commentary: New Testament* (IVP, 1993), 176.
5. "Prayer and Other Religious Practices," Pew Research Center, February 7, 2025, https://www.pewresearch.org/religion/2025/02/26/prayer-and-other-religious-practices/.
6. "We must remember the love of God, which ever desires only what is best for us. We must remember the wisdom of God, which alone knows what is best for us. We must remember the power of God, which alone can bring to pass that which is best for us. He who prays with a perfect trust in the love, wisdom and power of God will find God's peace." *Barclay's Daily Study Bible*, https://studylight.org/commentaries/eng/dsb/philippians-4.html.
7. Benjamin Schmolck, "My Jesus, as Thou Wilt!," (1704), Hymnary.org, https://hymnary.org/text/my_jesus_as_thou_wilt.
8. Charles Gabriel, "I Stand Amazed in the Presence," (1905).

Chapter 7: Managing the Disappointment of Unanswered Prayer

1. For the entire narrative, the ancient historian Josephus records both the defilement and the cleansing of the Temple (Josephus, *The Antiquities of the Jews* [Hendrickson, 1987], 322–88). Second Maccabees 6:2 specifically mentions the worship to Zeus.
2. The Voice of the Martyrs website: www.persecution.com.

Chapter 8: Getting Beyond Requests to God Himself

1. John Piper, *Desiring God: Meditations of a Christian Hedonist* (Multnomah, 2011), 10.
2. Henry Blackaby, Richard Blackaby, and Claude King, *Experiencing God* (B&H, 2008), 69.
3. John G. Paton, *Missionary to the New Hebrides: An Autobiography*, vol. 2 (Hodder and Sloughton, 1889), 11.

4. Jonathan Edwards, *Memoirs of the Rev. David Brainerd: Missionary to the Indians* (S. Converse, 1822), 50.
5. Ibid.
6. Ibid., 65.
7. Robert Burns, "Tam o'Shanter," Scottish Poetry Library, https://www.scottishpoetrylibrary.org.uk/poem/tam-o-shanter-tale/.
8. Bernard of Clairvaux, "Jesus, the Very Thought of Thee," Hymnary.org, https://hymnary.org/text/jesus_the_very_thought_of_thee.
9. Graham Kendrick, "Knowing You (All I Once Held Dear)," https://grahamkendrick.co.uk/knowing-you/.

Chapter 9: Why Pray If God Is in Control

1. C. S. Lewis, *The Screwtape Letters* (HarperOne, 2001), 148.

Appendix: Prayers for "Stuck" People

1. Arthur Bennett, ed., "God the All," in *The Valley of Vision* (Banner of Truth Trust, 2009), 4–5.
2. Arthur Bennett, ed., The Valley of Vision (Banner of Truth Trust, 2009), xxiv–xxv.